JESSE SHERA, LIBRARIANSHIP,
and INFORMATION SCIENCE

JESSE SHERA, LIBRARIANSHIP, AND INFORMTION SCIENCE

By

H. Curtis Wright

Library Juice Press
Sacramento, CA

Originally published as Occasional Research Paper Number 5, School of Information Sciences, Brigham Young University, 1988. Brigham Young University has generously granted us permission to republish the work in this volume.

Kathryn La Barre's Foreword and the Index by Victoria Jacobs are new to this edition, with the copyrights held by them, respectively, dated 2013.

Published by Library Juice Press, 2013

P.O. Box 188784
Sacramento, CA 95818

http://libraryjuicepress.com/

This book is printed on acid-free, sustainably-sourced paper.

Library of Congress Cataloging-in-Publication Data

Wright, H. Curtis (Herbert Curtis), 1928-2012.
  Jesse Shera, librarianship, and informtion science / by H. Curtis Wright.
      pages cm
  "Originally published by the Brigham Young University School of Library and Information Science in 1988, as number five in their Occasional Research Papers series"--Title page verso.
  Summary: "A biography of Jesse Hauk Shera, focusing on his role in defining and negotiating the boundaries of library science and information science, followed by a bibliography of his works"--Provided by publisher.
  Includes bibliographical references and index.
  ISBN 978-1-936117-75-8 (alk. paper)
 1. Shera, Jesse Hauk, 1903-1982. 2. Shera, Jesse Hauk, 1903-1982--Bibliography. 3. Librarians--United States--Biography. 4. Information scientists--United States--Biography. 5. Library science--United States--History--20th century. 6. Information science--United States--History--20th century. 7. Library science--Bibliography. 8. Information science--Bibliography. I. Title.
  Z720.S527W75 2013
  020.92--dc23

                                          2013006986

TABLE OF CONTENTS

Foreword   vii

1. *Shera's Professional Development*   1

2. *Shera's Computer and Machine Explorations*   13

3. *Bridging the Gap at Western Reserve*   21

4. *The Schism Between Information Science and Librarianship*   39

5. *Conclusion*   59

Chronological Bibliography.
The Published Works of Jesse Hauk Shera   61

Index   111

FOREWORD

One may well ask, "Why reissue this slender volume?" First published in small quantity as Occasional Research Paper, No. 5 in 1988 by the now closed School of Library and Information Sciences at Brigham Young University, this work is out of print and all but impossible to obtain. This question becomes especially pressing in light of a negative review in the *Journal of the American Society for Information Science*[1] which faults the author, H. Curtis Wright for substantially misrepresenting Jesse Hauk Shera's opinions [Chapter 4, 15 pp.], and which dismisses his biographical efforts [Chapter 1-3, 28 pp.] as a "run in attempt." The review omits reference to material that comprises nearly half of the volume, and which might provide one possible answer to this question. In addition to a biographical sketch, this work also contains a chronological bibliography of four hundred and eighty nine of Shera's publications [pp. 47-110]. In this effort, Wright aspires to but does not claim exhaustivity.

The bibliography begins with Shera's first publication in 1929 in his capacity as bibliographer at the Scripps Foundation for Research in Population Problems and ends - over forty pages and fifty seven years later - with several posthumous encyclopedia articles. Surely the depth and breadth of this effort was worth mentioning in a review published in one of the premier journals of information science? To underscore the central role of the bibliography, Wright indicates that it was compiled to provide order to his collection of *materica sherica*, "a ten foot stack of documents of Shera's personal papers, plus data from ancillary sources such as personal interviews." For Wright, the bibliography represents "the foundation upon which I shall try to reconstruct the portrait of an important life." (p.62).

This might occasion the appearance of another question, "Who was H. Curtis Wright, Shera's erstwhile biographer?" Wright received a dual PhD in Library Science and Greek Literature from Case Western University in 1969, during Shera's time as dean of the School of Library Science. Wright was a professor in the Department of Library and Information Sciences at Brigham Young University, Provo, Utah, until

---

[1] Margaret Anderson, "Review of Jesse Shera, Librarianship and Information Science," *Journal of the American Society for Information Science* 41 (April 1990): 211-212.

his retirement in 1993 when the school closed.[2] Wright's research focused upon the classics and drew from his deep foundation in philosophical and intellectual history. It would seem that the two men remained in contact and were familiar with each other's work throughout their professional lives. Shera wrote the preface for Wright's "dynamic, challenging, readable, and sometimes amusing" philosophical, epistemological and sociological study of Greek librarianship before and after the introduction of writing.[3] Additionally, Wright's own arguments form the centerpiece of a response article written by Shera just two months prior to his death (in 1982)[4] to Rayward's reflection chapter: "Library and Information Sciences: Disciplinary Differentiation, Competition, and Convergence" in Machlup and Mansfield's book, *The Study of Information, Interdisciplinary Messages*.[5]

Wright's contribution, in addition to providing a bibliographical map of the breadth and depth of Shera's writings, stands alone as the sole book-length study of Shera's life and career. An early manuscript of the present work, "Shera as a Bridge Between Librarianship and Information Science" appears in the *Journal of Library History*.[6] Though admittedly imperfect, this biography merits consideration, and can more fully inform assessment of Shera's contributions to the intellectual foundations of the still but steadily evolving field of library

---

[2] Herbert Curtis Wright. "Obituaries" *Daily Herald*, Provo, Utah . January 25, 2012 12:50 am. Online:
http://www.heraldextra.com/lifestyles/announcements/obituaries/herbert-curtis-wright/article_753a25b4-547e-5509-a814-1e98571e7c85.html

[3] *The Oral Antecedents of Greek Librarianship*, Brigham Young University Press, 1977. 237 p.

[4] Jesse H. Shera, "Librarianship and Information Science," in *The Study of Information, Interdisciplinary Messages*, Fritz Machlup and Una Mansfield, John Wiley, 1983: 379-388.

[5] H. Curtis Wright, "Wrong Way to Go," Journal of the American Society for Information Science, 30 (March 1979): 67-76, and "Inquiry in Science and Librarianship," Journal of Library History 13 no. 3 (Summer 1978): 250-264, and "Jesse H. Shera, "Librarianship and Information Science," in *The Study of Information, Interdisciplinary Messages*, Fritz Machlup and Una Mansfield, John Wiley, 1983: 379-388.

[6] "Shera as a bridge between Librarianship and Information Science," *Journal of Library History* 20, No. 2 (Spring 1985): 137-156.

and information science (LIS). The biography-seeking reader will find that this volume does not read in a straightforward fashion, though the first three chapters provide an adequate summary. The strength of these chapters lie in the fact that Wright allows Shera speak for himself by drawing heavily upon excerpts from oral history interviews conducted by Ruderman (a masters student) in 1968 and by Helmuth (an archivist at Case Western) in 1970.[7] For those deeply interested in detailed chronicles and accountings of achievements – a visit to Shera's entries in *Current Biography* and *American National Biography Online* should suffice for now.[8] Quite intriguingly, Wright's introduction to the bibliography in this volume indicates that he is drawing from a nearly complete set of Shera's papers that may well extend the holdings that comprise the Papers of Jesse Hauk Shera (1903–1982), at Case Western Reserve University Archives. In 2018, Wright's own papers, which might include his heavily annotated *materia sherica*, will be opened to examination by researchers.[9]

One might ask a penultimate question, "Who was Jesse Shera?" Gadfly? Scholar? Raconteur? In keeping with Wright's approach, I will let Shera speak for himself. Long a staunch advocate for the social and humanistic enterprise of librarianship and one whom many have called the bridge between librarianship and information science, he brought this ethos to his editorial duties at *American Documentation*. In 1952, he speaks to documentalists who are,[10]

---

[7] Mrs. Gerald Ruderman. Tape recording. Papers of Jesse Hauk Shera (1903–1982), series 27DD5, box 52. Case Western Reserve University Archives, Cleveland, OH. Conducted as part of: Laurie P. Ruderman, "Jesse Shera: A Bio-Bibliography" (master's thesis, Kent State Univ., 1968). Ruth Helmuth. Tape recording and transcript. Papers of Jesse Hauk Shera (1903–1982).

[8] "Jesse H. Shera," *Current Biography, (Bio. Ref. Bank)*,(June 1964), (June 1, 1982): *Current Biography Illustrated (H.W. Wilson)*. Web. 8 Dec. 2012. Jenny Presnell. "Shera, Jesse Hauk": http://www.Anb.org/articles/20/10-01172.html; *American National Biography Online* Feb. 2000. Web. 8 Dec. 2012.

[9] UA 5443; Library School Collection of H. Curtis Wright papers; University Archives; L. Tom Perry Special Collections, Harold B. Lee Library, Brigham Young University.

[10] Shera, "Needed Creative Documentation," *American Documentation*, 7 (2), 1956, ii.

> ...engaged in a grim struggle for mastery of the written word, a struggle upon which the very survival of our society may depend. When culture is set against culture we cannot afford to lose our way in the wilderness of our own communication system...Documentation is not a self marketing commodity; our task is often as much education al and promotional as it is investigatory for, in a democracy, any branch of esoteric knowledge must arouse a reasonable degree of popular acceptance if it is to prosper and thrive. "

He is also a staunch advocate for the importance of fundamental research,[11]

> The ancient aphorism that history does not repeat itself, but historians repeat each other is, unfortunately, applicable to documentalists...
>
> We cannot advance for the simple reason that we are lost as to the direction which such advances should take... Documentalists are very near to being surfeited ... with demands for immediate and specific solutions to problems that are equally immediate and specific. The only true solution to our difficulties lies in ... support for fundamental research ... Where there is no vision a profession cannot prosper. A sedulous dedication to the exploration of fundamentals is vital to documentation, and indeed it is this that distinguishes the true profession from the craft.

In "A mandate for documentalists,"[12] he refers to a passage from an E.B. White article in the *New Yorker* about the need for documentalists to put time and energy,

> ... into launching our best missile – our ideas. We should flood the world with the good books that make men's hearts catch fire. We should not expect the man in the Antipodes to travel to the corner of Forty-second street and Fifth avenue and search through the card catalog... In this the documentalist and the librarian find a common responsibility and a common task. In the total communication process their roles are essentially

---

[11] Shera, "Fundamental Research, A Few Fundamentals," *American Documentation*, 7(3) (March 1956): ii.

[12] Shera, *American Documentation*, 11 (4), (April 1960): ii.

> one, they are the mediators between man and the graphic records of the human adventure... they are... true internationalists... The catalogues, the codes, the computers of the documentalist are very powerful and useful tools to supplement the innate capabilities of man, but alone they can never completely untangle the web of human communication, nor can they fully solve the problems of human misunderstanding... To see that man is not stifled by his own records, to see that the Letter does not kill, to see that the book is always at the service of the humanist, to be the statement of their own world of graphic communication – that is the imperative for all librarians and documentalists everywhere; that is their mandate for the decades of the "sixties."

In top form as raconteur he challenged LIS to come to grips with reality,

> It was the best of times, it was the worst of times, it was the age of wisdom, it was the age of foolishness, it was the epoch of belief, it was the epoch of incredulity, it was the season of Light, it was the season of Darkness, it was the spring of hope, it was the winter of despair, we had everything before us, we had nothing before us, we were all going direct to Heaven, we were all going direct the other way - in short, the period was so far like the present period, that some of its noisiest authorities insisted on its being received, for good or for evil, in the superlative degree of comparison only.[13]

Shera's unwavering focus on the necessity of an intellectual foundation remained through the waxing and waning of documentation and well into the ascendency of LIS. The notion of social epistemology[14] – which emphasizes the importance of the sociological dimensions of knowledge, anchored this agenda. Originally the vision of Margaret Egan, Shera ensured that this notion outlived her untimely death in 1959 – though he was not always careful to credit her.[15] In

---

[13] Shera, "The Librarian and the Machine" (originally published June 15, 1961) in *Library Journal*.

[14] Margaret Egan and Jesse Shera, 1952. "Foundations of a Theory of Bibliography." *Library Quarterly* 44: 125-37. (1952)

[15] Furner, Jonathan. 2004. "'A Brilliant Mind': Margaret Egan and Social Epistemology." *Library Trends* 52(4):792-809.

1970, Shera delivered a series of reflections about the drastic changes then facing librarianship that drew out the dual themes of the importance of service in librarianship, and the role social epistemology could play in providing a firm intellectual foundation that best reflects the situated nature of librarianship in communication, language, human behavior, culture, and society. Within such a worldview, the library is an agent of society, and the librarian seeks to communicate the importance of knowledge to both individuals and society. Social epistemology forms the theoretical structure that knits together contributions of psychology, epistemology, and sociology into a fully tinterdisciplinary approach to the study of knowledge and intellectual processes in society. In these lectures, Shera posits, crediting Egan, that social epistemology with its focus upon the "production, flow, integration, and consumption of all forms of communicated thought throughout the entire social fabric...giv[es] rise to a new synthesis of the interaction between knowledge and social activity... necessarily form[ing] the theoretical basis of the practice of librarianship as it grapples with the influence of knowledge on society."[16] Only with social epistemology at the heart of librarianship, can a librarian fulfill,

> effective management of the transcript...the graphic records of society...its values as well as its facts, its imagery as well as its reality. The librarian is at once historical, contemporary, and anticipatory...once we have made some headway...in developing this discipline...we will not need to worry any longer about whether or not there is a library science..."[17]

That may leave the reader with one final question, "How, and in what ways might this volume help extend understanding of the relevance of Shera's work to the broader discussion of the role of LIS in the information professions?" A complex and nuanced terrain indeed! In his essay "Librarianship and Information Science,"[18] Shera reflects on the early days of the American Documentation Institute (ADI) and then prevalent argumentation in favor of changing the appellation 'library school' to 'school of documentation'. Here, Shera

---

[16] Shera, "Sociological Foundations of Librarianship" *Sarada Ranganathan Endowment for Library Science*. (1970): 85-88.

[17] Ibid, p. 87.

[18] Shera in *The Study of Information, Interdisciplinary Messages,* Fritz Machlup and Una Mansfield, John Wiley, 1983: 379-388.

muses about the existence or absence of organic interdisciplinarity between library and information science, and makes a stark admission. He no longer believes, as he once did, that information science is capable of "providing the intellectual and theoretical foundations of librarianship." He even questions the existence of interdisciplinarity, as he sees instead "only a series of borrowings of the technology of one for the use of another." By deploying Wright's argument "our schools of library science are busily engaged in producing 'control artists' who consistently mistake symbol for reality and believe that counting or figuring with these symbols solves the bibliographic access problem,"[19] Shera cautions that librarians:

> [H]ave become so concerned with process that they have confused substance with instrumentation. Processing data can be performed by machine, but only the human mind can process knowledge or even information. Information science is based on data and their manipulation, not on ideas.[20]

Shera advocates fighting for recognition of the deep knowledge librarians possess with his now famous quote:

> The computer is here to stay, therefore it must be kept in its proper place as a tool and a slave, or we will become sorcerer's apprentices, with data, data everywhere and not a thought to think.[21]

He damns the haste with which library science "'seized upon information science' as potential supports to professionalism ... [for] science does not a profession make, and an overlay of scientific operations is not a sine qua non for professionalism." His concerns with the consequences of sublimating librarianship to the lure of the machine in favor of emerging technologies represents,

> the loss of control of the library profession to other and less competent hands. Of the dangers in this threat we do not seem to be fully aware....If we permit ourselves to be mesmerized by

---

[19] H. Curtis Wright "Instrumentality of Data" in *National Library Association Newsletter*, vol. 6 (May 1981), pp. 4-5.

[20] Shera, op cit., p. 384.

[21] Ibid.

the gadget, if we accept the flickering image of data on a fluorescent screen as knowledge, we will soon become like those mythical people of many centuries ago who mistook for reality the passing shadows reflected on the walls of a cave.[22]

This call to arms from thirty years ago still resonates deeply in the context of the iSchool phenomenon. Formally founded in 2005, the internationally-focused iSchool organization counts thirty-six schools among its members.[23] The discipline of LIS no longer engages in discussions of whether or not to abandon 'library' for 'documentation' as in the 60s and 70s. Instead some iSchools seek to substitute 'information' for 'library' in newly designed institutional heraldry, in a move which some see as a final repudiation of any connection between information science and librarianship.

The iSchool purpose statement is as follows:

> The iSchools take it as given that expertise in all forms of information is required for progress in science, business, education, and culture. This expertise must include understanding of the uses and users of information, the nature of information itself, as well as information technologies and their applications. iSchools promote an interdisciplinary approach to understanding the opportunities and challenges of information management, with a core commitment to concepts like universal access and user-centered organization of information. The field is concerned broadly with questions of design and preservation across information spaces, from digital and virtual spaces such as online communities, social networking, the World Wide Web, and databases to physical spaces such as libraries, museums, collections, and other repositories.[24]

Much in line with Shera's writings, the iSchools vision statement invokes the beauty of "interdisciplinary approaches to harnessing the power of information and technology, and maximizing the potential of

---

[22] Ibid, p. 387.

[23] "About the iSchools" Web. 8 Dec. 2012. Eleven members are located outside of North America.

[24] Ibid.

humans." By providing "innovative systems" and "information solutions that benefit individuals, organizations, and society" the organization anticipates that iSchool graduates will work "in many different types and sizes of organizations", and impact both society and policy "locally and internationally."[25] This new movement was born at a time when Shera's beloved ADI was declining in strength and membership. First known as the American Documentation Institute (1937- 1969), it became the American Society for Information Science & Technology in 1996, and in 2013 it will become the Association for Information Science & Technology to better reflect a renewed focus on international concerns.[26] Wherever one might situate the connection or discontinuity of the relation between librarian and information scientist, or whatever might be the eventual outcome in the battle between ASIS&T and the iSchools, Shera's words give hope to the besieged librarian that are as true today as when he wrote them in 1969,

> Because librarianship is facing some very critical years which may well decide its future course, we hope that those responsible for the professional education of tomorrow's librarians will learn from the mistakes of the past, and prepare the student to understand his proper place in the changing environment created by 'all these new things,' a world in which everything he has learned about the *how* of librarianship may be overthrown before he has lived out his professional life, a world in which only the *why* is the eternal veracity.[27]

And as John Berry notes in Shera's obit, can any librarian not be inspired by the following message:

> To keep something burning, to carry the light as best we can forward into the darkness and wind: That good friends, is the apotheosis of librarianship, that is what librarianship is all about. To bring man and book together in a fruitful relationship for

---

[25] Ibid.

[26] Irene Farkas-Conn in From Documentation to Information Science: The Beginnings and Early Development of the American Documentation Institute – American Society for Information Science (Greenwood, 1990). "Results of recent vote regarding ASIS&T's name" by Diane Sonnenwald. [Internal membership posting] 10-12-2012 on asist-announce listserv.

[27] Shera, editorial *Wilson Library Bulletin*, (April 1968): 156.

the benefit of the individual, and through the individual to society, and to do so in an environment hospitable to serious meditation; that is our task ... to carry the light as best we can, even though it may be no more than a candle in the window that proclaims the library as a storage place for the memory of the human race; a place for the soft rustle of pages and the quiet stir of thought.[28]

This then, is the true contribution of Wright's effort – to keep the candle of interest in Shera burning brightly, and to provide a map by which to explore the vast terrain of his intellectual contributions to library and information science. My recommendation is to explore freely and drink deeply from Shera's legacy!

~ Kathryn La Barre
Associate Professor, Graduate School of Library and Information Science , University of Illinois at Urbana-Champaign

---

[28] Shera, "The Quiet Stir of Thought," *Library Journal,* (September 1969): 2875. John Berry, "Shera's Rich Legacy," *Library Journal* (April 1982): 663.

Science has . . . been so successful that it has . . . earned a great and strange reputation. If it has never yet been defeated, presumably it is all-powerful. And since science is, after all, the work of scientists...then presumably these scientists are both so clever and so wise that *they* can do anything. Perhaps we should turn the world over to this superbreed . . . . Perhaps they could solve all problems of human relations, of economic stability, of international peace, and of the good life. Perhaps they should design not only the churches, but the creeds also. Perhaps the best music and . . . poetry *will*, in a short time, come out of a machine. The sad fact is that some scientists themselves appear to believe precisely this. And this arrogant attitude . . . irritates, or even angers, the social scientists, the humanists, the moralists, and the creative artists.

Warren Weaver[29]

---

[29] Warren Weaver, "The Imperfections of Science," *American Scientist* 49 (1961): 101. Italics his.

CHAPTER ONE
SHERA'S PROFESSIONAL DEVELOPMENT[30]

An Unusual Beginning

Jesse Shera has called his entry into librarianship "an act of desperation," the result of a decision "which the library profession has lived to regret."[31] It was an agonizing decision, because "Shera did not grow up with the idea of being a librarian."[32] He wanted to be a scientist in the early twenties, and from his high school years through a year or more of college, his closest friends were interested in scientific careers. His good friend Winfield Heckert, for example, went into chemistry, and Shera wanted to do likewise. But that, he says, was not to be.

> I wanted to be a chemist....
>
> In high school, I thought I was going to go [into chemistry]. I took quite a block of chemistry [in those days], and I even took some chemistry in college. I was [deeply] interested in chemistry....
>
> And then I got into a course in quantitative analysis, and I found out my eyes were going to be a [terrible] handicap when it came to handling such things as analytical balances, and I might as well give up....

---

[30] The influence of Jesse Shera on modern librarianship has been profound. He transformed the traditional library school at Western Reserve University into a sophisticated educational operation, he was a charter member of what later became the American Society for Information Science, and he was one of the first in the profession to foresee the potential of computers for library operations. He originally desired to be a scientist and had extensive training in the social sciences; yet he came to dispute the supremacy of science in the field of librarianship. He believed that librarianship is a humanistic profession that can not and should not be scientifically controlled or designed; that information science is useful in achieving library goals but does not constitute an end in itself. This monograph will explore Shera's life and attitudes, focusing on his idea of the proper roles of information science and librarianship.
[31] *Current Biography*, 1964, 409.
[32] Margaret Kaltenback, "Biography Jesse Shera" TMs, Archives, Case Western University, Cleveland, Ohio. This manuscript was submitted to the editor of the *ALA world Encyclopedia of Library and Information Services*, and was published there in a severely shortened form as "Shera, Jesse H.".

So, I dropped it. But I have always been . . . interested in science.³³

Next, Shera tells us, "I had a brief period of flirtation with sociology and social science."³⁴ This flirtation was important, although he never actually became a social scientist: it was to be "reflected in his master's thesis at Yale" (on the sociological aspects of Galsworthy's Forsyte novels), enhanced by Warren S. Thompson, "Director of the Scripps Foundation who held a Ph.D. in sociology from Columbia," encouraged by the Graduate Library School (GLS) at Chicago, and expressed one way or another in virtually everything he published.³⁵ Shera has portrayed this glimmering interest in social science against the backdrop of an early distaste for the library profession.

First Impressions of Librarianship

> 'The new librarian,' I confided to my family in . . . 1923, 'is a real grouch.' The verdict was personal, prejudiced, and . . . emphatic. . . . I had been comfortably seated in the . . . Library, with my feet propped on a convenient table, while . . . reading . . . E. A. Ross' *Introduction to Sociology* . . . . The object of my . . . derision was Edgar Weld King . . . .
>
> My occupation with the 'science of society' was interrupted when . . . [he] stopped to inform me . . . that the posture I had assumed was not appropriate to a dignified scholar. . . . King moved on . . . only to return . . . [and] ask if I had a stack permit. I produced the card with an arrogant flourish and he went his way, leaving me to grumble . . . about librarians in general and this one in particular.³⁶

---

³³ Jesse Shera, Interviews by Ruth Helmuth, 1970, and Mrs. Gerald H. Ruderman, 1968, transcripts in Case Western Reserve Archives, Cleveland, Ohio. Shera adds that "I never had real close contact with the physical scientists . . . I've done quite a lot of reading in science, but the field has changed so [dramatically] that I feel utterly inadequate," Shera, Interview by Ruderman, 1968 Mrs. Helmuth is the university archivist at Case Western Reserve University. Mrs. Ruderman was a student in library science at Kent State University in 1968.
³⁴ Shera, Interview by Helmuth, 1970.
³⁵ Margaret Kaltenbach, "Shera, Jesse Hauk," *ALA World Encyclopedia of Library and Information Services*, ed. R. Wedgeworth (Chicago: American Library Association, 1980): 525.
³⁶ Jesse H. Shera, "King of Miami: an Appreciation," *Ohio Library Association Bulletin* 50 (1980): 14.

Within five years, that 'grumpy old librarian'[37] would open the gates of librarianship to this budding scholar. Edgar Weld King subsequently became one of the key people in the personal and professional life of Jesse Hauk Shera. It is impossible to overestimate the importance of his influence on Shera. But clearly, as a sophomore in the early twenties, Shera had no use for King or for his profession.

Humanist College Training

So, Shera turned to the humanities. "And then," he says, "I really got down to what I liked, which was English literature."[38] To make a long story short, he graduated with honors in English literature from Miami University in 1925, and "went off to Yale" where he had an exhilarating experience with the same subject.

> I mean, here I was, a kid who had lived all his life in Oxford, a little town in southwestern Ohio with about 2,500 population . . . . And for the first time, I was thrown into a major university with a distinguished faculty . . . . They were really distinguished people, and I got terribly excited. I just ran around like a cat with half a dozen saucers of cream, lapping this up. And I came out with a master's degree in 1927.[39]

During the Yale period, he says, "my only interest was in becoming a Professor of English literature." He was "rather anti-library," as a matter of fact, because he had formed "the impression that librarians generally knew very little about the *insides* of books." He therefore "developed no interest either in libraries or library history at Yale."[40]

By graduation time, however, his aspirations were thwarted by formidable obstacles, which included "some serious reservations" about pursuing English literature as a career.[41] "If there had been a

---

[37] "Years later, when 'Ned' and I had become close friends, I reminded him of the incident, which he . . . had completely forgotten. I added, 'Before I knew you I thought you were a grumpy old librarian.' His response was . . . , 'Before you knew me perhaps I was,'" ibid.
[38] Shera, Interview by Helmuth (1970).
[39] Ibid.
[40] Jesse Shera to Michael Harris, 19 September 1974. Italics his.
[41] See Herman H. Fussler, "Jesse Hauk Shera," memorial service address, 16 March 1982, TMs [photocopy], Archives, Case Western University, Cleveland, Ohio. Cf. Shera's remarks in Shera Interview by Ruderman (1968): "I've been able to do more in librarianship than I ever would have done teaching Shakespeare. I still love to get off

good opening in English teaching," he admits, "I'd have gone to it."[42] But conditions were bad in 1927: there were no openings anywhere-- the coming Depression had already seen to that. "There were just too many teachers around with all their faculties who wanted jobs."[43]

Turns to Librarianship

It must have seemed like the end of the road for Shera. He had gone from the physical sciences to the social sciences because of impaired vision, and from the social sciences to the humanities where he found his first love. Now he was forced again, this time by an impending Depression and poor eyesight to go somewhere else. "So, I went back to Oxford," he tells us, "and talked to Raymond M. Hughes, the President of Miami University."[44]

He was seeking counsel from a distinguished friend. Jess was raised in a small university town, where most of the professors, including R. M. Hughes, had taken an early liking to him. Hughes had been a professor of chemistry at Miami from 1904 to 1913 (from Shera's first to tenth years of life) when he became President of the university. And in 1927, shortly before he left Miami for the presidency of Iowa State University, Jess had sought him out.

During one of their conversations, as they discussed limited academic opportunities in a vicious economic climate, a thought occurred to Shera. "What about librarianship?" he asked. "And President Hughes said, "That's a good idea. I'd never thought of that. I'm going to send you over to see King."[45] So Hughes contacted "Ned" King, as "Miami's first professionally trained librarian"[46] was known to his friends, and Jess made an appointment to see him. The ensuing interview marked a turning point in Shera's life. "English teachers . . . were a dime a dozen," he later recalled," and with my visual handicap the outlook was quite discouraging. Therefore I turned to librarianship,

---

with Shakespeare . . . . But my old graduate work in English honors, I have to admit, was pretty stultifying, really. What can you do with it? We've handled and sandpapered the bones of Shakespeare until there's nothing left . . . . You can't spend all your time teaching English and telling how wonderful *Hamlet* is, even though you know darn well it *is* wonderful."

[42] Shera, Interview by Ruderman (1968).
[43] Shera, Interview by Helmuth (1970).
[44] Ibid.
[45] Shera, Interview by Helmuth (1970).
[46] Shera, "King of Miami," 14.

and now know that my 'misfortune' was probably a blessing in disguise."[47]

First Position

> I went over and talked to Ned. And he said, 'Well, I don't have any place in the budget for you now, but I've got part-time work. If you're willing to work on an hourly basis, I've got a good hourly budget: you can put in as many hours as you want, and as soon as something opens up, I'd be glad to have you with your English background.[48]

So Shera went to work at an hourly wage "as Assistant Cataloger in the Miami University Library for the academic year of 1927-28."[49] This position, Fussler observes, "was probably not the most exciting intellectual activity . . . a Yale M.A. in English . . . could . . . imagine."[50] Yet, Shera did find excitement in it. His title, Assistant Cataloger, is misleading, for he was far from being a narrow specialist with a particular task. He became the librarian's apprentice, a kind of "substitute Ned King," more or less, who worked all over the library and gained experience in every aspect of the business.[51] "It was Ned King," he says, "who . . . introduced me to librarianship."[52]

> I never went through the first year of library school at all. But he just had me work at all sorts of places all over that library. I worked at the reference desk, and the circulation desk, and the reserve room. I worked as a kind of administrative assistant to him, although I didn't have that title. I did all kinds of things. I was shifted from one thing to another, and it was . . . tremendous.[53]

> The experience he gave me during one short year as his administrative assistant was far greater than I could have gained . . . [from] a first year of library school. Without then realizing it, I was seeing the old apprentice system at its best,

---

[47] Ibid.; and Shera to Harris (1974).
[48] Shera, Interview by Helmuth (1970).
[49] Fussler, Memorial address for Shera.
[50] Ibid.
[51] The title was apparently an administrative maneuver to get Shera on the payroll.
[52] Shera, "King of Miami," 14.
[53] Shera, Interview by Helmuth (1970).

and I have wished many times that my students could have had such a beginning exposure to librarianship.[54]

There is no doubt about it: this year with Edgar Weld King was a very important year in the life of Jesse Shera.[55] It was the crucial year of his agonizing decision to turn away from English literature and embrace librarianship. And thinking back in 1968 on that painful crossroads, he was to say: "I think the Lord was on my side, although I didn't know it at the time."[56]

Thwarted Library School Plans

So Shera worked at librarianship for a year under Ned King, learning the business from the inside out. It is clear, despite his initial reservations, that he "was not turned away from libraries and related systems of information access by this experience."[57] During that year, King had encouraged him to go to library school, and he made plans to attend King's old school at Columbia.[58]

> I did enroll at Columbia and was accepted . . . . Then one day, Warren S. Thompson, who was Director of the Scripps Foundation for Population Research at Miami . . . . needed a librarian. They'd had an old gal who'd been librarian, and she had retired, and the library was in an awful mess."[59]

When approached by Thompson about needing a librarian, King told him, "I've got just the man for you, but he won't be available for another year because he's going to Columbia."[60] Thompson replied, "Well, I want somebody now. I don't want to wait a year, and I don't care whether he has a library degree . . . or not."[61] King then told Shera about this, because something promising had opened up.

---

[54] Shera, "King of Miami," 14.
[55] R. M. Hughes and others were actively seeking employment for Shera, and he would undoubtedly have been lost to librarianship if they had been successful in their searches.
[56] Shera, Interview by Ruderman 1968. Also cited in the Kaltenbach Ms.
[57] Fussler, Memorial Address for Shera.
[58] Shera, Interview by Ruderman (1968). "I've always been amused because when I was talking to King about a place to go, naturally he favored Columbia, having been there himself. I mentioned Western Reserve and he said 'Oh, you don't want to go there-- only girls go to Western Reserve,'" ibid.
[59] Ibid.
[60] Shera, Interview by Helmuth (1970).
[61] Shera, Interviews by Helmuth and Ruderman (1970, 1968).

He said, 'Why don't you go in and talk to Thompson anyway?' And I did. And Thompson said [again], 'I don't care if you have a library degree or not. I just want somebody who can do the job.' And I thought about it, and I said to Ned, 'Well, this is the kind of job I'd like after I leave Columbia. Why bother with Columbia?'[62]

He also wanted to get married, and working with Thompson would mean a financial boost to support the marriage. "So," he says, "I scotched up my plans to go to Columbia."[63] And with that, Shera withdrew his application for library school, accepted employment with Thompson, "and started in right then and there."[64] A few months later, on 3 November 1928, he and Helen Bickham were married; and from 1928 to 1938 they sat out the depression in Oxford, Ohio, where Jess worked for ten years at the Scripps Foundation for Population Research.[65]

Social Science Library Experience

Shera now went to work at librarianship from the outside in. He became in effect a "research librarian" to Warren S. Thompson, and his job plunged him deeply into the kinds of library research that helped Thompson pull materials on population problems together and compile his books.[66] There is every reason to believe that "Jesse found this position attractive," for "working directly with . . . a competent research organization . . . [in] addressing . . . complex and serious problems can . . . be a very enlightening and intellectually stimulating experience."[67] It was here that Shera built his reputation as a population specialist and became an expert statistician and bibliographer. "During that period," he tells us, "I became seriously interested in library work, [and] specifically in special libraries."[68]

---

[62] Shera, Interview by Helmuth (1970). See also the parallel account in the Interview by Ruderman (1968).
[63] Shera, Interview by Ruderman (1968).
[64] Shera, Interview by Helmuth (1970).
[65] Shera, Interview by Ruderman (1968). "The depression didn't bother me like it did a lot of people, because I had good solid employment there at this Foundation," Shera, Interview with Helmuth (1970).
[66] Thompson mentions Shera in this role in several of his books.
[67] Fussler, Memorial address for Shera.
[68] Shera, Interview by Ruderman (1968).

Effects of Shera's Background

Shera's library experiences at Miami, which followed his Master's degree at Yale and preceded his doctoral studies at Chicago, constitute the fertile seedbed in which the accomplishments of his productive life took root and bore fruit. We note here only three aspects of his ideal work situations with King and Thompson.

1. <u>Effects of backdoor entrance</u>. It is apparent, first of all, that Shera entered the library profession through the back door, bypassing library school altogether. "I just kind of backed into the thing," he says, "and practiced librarianship for eleven years before I actually went to library school" as a doctoral student in the GLS at Chicago.[69] That fact had created the paradox of a fortune deficiency in Shera's education. "It was probably a good thing I never went to the first year of library school," he says, because "it freed me from some of the stuff that students in those days went through."[70]

He thus avoided, certainly, the heavy hand of library traditionalism (which is still running and ruining the profession) and became one of its severest critics. But later, as a library educator, it also gave him pause. When asked if his were not the easier of two ways to enter librarianship he replied, "Well, it is, yes. And of course, it does make you wonder sometimes, if you run a library education program, when you know it can be done the other way."[71] So, having entered by the "wrong" way himself, he sought all his days to make the "right" way truly meaningful.[72]

2. <u>Effects of comprehensiveness</u>. Shera took from King a cosmopolitan view of the profession which made him a citizen of librarianship in the most comprehensive of all possible senses. He became a librarian's

---

[69] Ibid. Cited also, with slight variations, by Kaltenbach, "Shera, Jesse Hauk," 525, and in her Ms. for that article.

[70] Shera, Interview by Helmuth (1970).

[71] Shera, Interview by Ruderman (1968, adding that "we [library educators] do more 'educating' than we need to."

[72] "I backed into it, just as you did," Shera told his interviewer, who had gone into librarianship because she couldn't make it in English. "It's unfortunate," he added. "I mean, this isn't the way you get good people--even as good as you and I are. That's not the best way to get them. We're accidents . . . . the fact remains that . . . [our coming into librarianship] was a coincidence, a fortuitous kind of thing." When asked further if there was any way to cause more "fortuitous accidents," he replied: "I think so, because I still can't help thinking that if librarianship were presented in the right way it could arouse a lot of interest," Shera, Interview by Ruderman (1968).

librarian: nothing in the world of librarianship was foreing to him, and little escaped his notice. He roved over every nook and cranny of Miami's libraries in the early days; and then he wandered ceaselessly over the length and breadth of the library profession, roaming its main thoroughfares, exploring its side streets and back alleys, and tipping over all of its garbage cans.

He was the very antithesis of the *Fachidioten*, those "excessively specialized experts" ignorant of everything outside their specialties.[73] "I've been one of those creatures," he says, "who has dabbled around in a whole lot of things."[74] And he never gave up his relentless search for a holistic philosophy of librarianship that would tie all of its details and loose ends together.

3. Effects of user-orientation. Ten years of researching with Thompson and the Scripps Foundation reinforced in Shera his instinctive acceptance of the user's point of view in librarianship. A potent factor in creating this point of view was his poor eyesight, which had plagued him from birth: he had to compensate for it even as a child. "But Jesse didn't like to talk about that . . . . He had this handicap, and he had to overcome it, and that was that."[75] He had learned a very early age to pretend that he could see as well as anybody else; and he often convinced people of this.[76]

He learned also, as an important part of his strategy for feigning normal vision, to get interested in whatever interested his friends by keeping himself informed on such things as baseball scores, stock market reports, and what the politicians were saying. He saw to it, in short, that he always had something interesting to talk about with anyone he was likely to meet. And the best measure of his success, perhaps, is his daughter, Mary, who, as a young girl, was totally unconcerned about her father's visual handicap.[77] This interest in others surfaced quite naturally in his vision of librarianship. He was not impressed with the library *profession* when he graduated from Yale. But, he says, "I had always been interested in libraries;" and when asked if

---

[73] Fritz Machlup and Una Mansfield, "Cultural Diversity in Studies of Information," in *The Study of Information; Interdisciplinary Messages*, Fritz Machlup and Una Mansfield, eds. (New York: Wiley, 1983), 5.
[74] Shera, Interview by Ruderman (1968).
[75] John S. Millis, Interview by W. K. Cawley, 27 June 1983. Taperecorded transcript, Archives, Case Western Reserve University, Cleveland, Ohio.
[76] This is confirmed by his family and by several of his boyhood friends.
[77] Mary (Shera) Baum. Interview by H. Curtis Wright, 13 September 1984.

that interest was "purely from the student's point of view," he answered: "Yes, that's right. It was from the user's point of view."[78]

Shera knew that the librarian lives by serving the informational interests of other people. That's why he argued in 1934 that the reference function of librarianship is successful only when the librarian understands, completely and without distortion, the patron's point of view.[79] That is also why he insisted in 1944 that administration is a means for attaining nonadministrative ends, not a means for attaining its own ends, or a means without ends.[80] That's how he remembered the library at Miami in 1966--as "a constant invitation to reading and an aid to scholarship."[81] And that, according to John S. Millis, President Emeritus of Western Reserve University and Shera's close personal friend, is also how he ended his days in 1982. When asked what he discussed with Shera near the end of his life during frequent visits to the hospital, Millis responded:

> These conversations were not very long, because I didn't want to tire him. I'd go there every day, for maybe fifteen minutes, something of that sort. He was very much interested in what I had been doing at that particular time. If I had been away on some out-of-town excursion, he'd ask, and I would report, how things were down at the University of Texas, or at Arizona or Minnesota or wherever I had been, or what I had learned about psychometrics, for example, on a recent trip to Philadelphia.
>
> Now that you're asking, it sounds kind of selfish, doesn't it, to be talking about my affairs rather than his. But I think that was the way he wanted it. Occasionally, he would turn the conversation to his own physical condition--the doctor's reports, and so on. But generally, he wanted to talk about what

---

[78] Shera, Interview by Ruderman (1968).
[79] Jesse Shera, "Viewpoint Shift in Reference Work," *Special Libraries* 25 (1934): 235-37. "In so far as the librarian sees the problem through the eyes of him whom he serves, by so much will his usefulness and efficiency be increased . . . . The . . . successful special librarian must know much more than mere literature of his subject; he must know the minds of his patrons, understand their . . . mental reactions, [and] develop . . . parallel mental associations," ibid., 237.
[80] Jesse H. Shera, "Special Library Objectives and their Relation to Administration," *Special Libraries* 35 (1944): 91-94. "The cardinal sin of the administrator is a . . . propensity to forget that . . . [administration] is never an end in itself, but . . . a means to . . . the attainment of some superior objective . . . When administrative policies come into conflict with the aims and purposes of the enterprise it serves, these policies must give way . . . . The administration of any . . . enterprise cannot be considered apart from the larger objectives of that enterprise," ibid., 91-92.
[81] Jesse H. Shera, "Without Reserve," *Wilson Library Bulletin* 41 (1966): 89.

I was doing. That's in character, you know. Jesse was very much interested in other people as people. And the last thing you'd expect him to do was to have been bitter about his physical condition and the prospect of ever getting well, which was nil. So his last days were in character with the rest of his life.[82]

---

[82] Millis, Interview by Cawley, 27 June 1983.

CHAPTER 2
SHERA'S MACHINE AND COMPUTER EXPLORATIONS

Early Interest in Machines

Before and during high school, Jess was fascinated with carpentry. The manual tools he used in those days have been preserved by his family, and there are lots of them: mitre boxes, saws of various kinds, squares, hammers, plumb bobs, and so on.[83] Clearly "he had great interest in tools as a boy, and some desire to follow it up."[84] He expressed it later, too--by helping his wife make their daughter a doll bed from a picture, for example.[85]

It is also clear that he was fascinated with intellectual tools, because "he was always interested in how people communicate with one another. He was very much interested in the operations of the mind in this--why man was able to communicate in ways not utilized by animals."[86] These interests in manual and intellectual tools combined at an early age to form his deep interest in communications technology, which grew progressively stronger as he became a researcher at the Scripps Foundation, a graduate student in the GLS, an intelligence officer in the OSS (Office of Strategic Services), and a professor of library science at the GLS.

Recognition of Computer Needs in Libraries

At the Scripps Foundation in the thirties, Shera was constantly "doing . . . population studies." He therefore "did a great deal of statistical work, particularly in the forecasting of population growth," which brought him into "considerable contact with tabulating machines."[87] These were the old Hollerith machines, which were invented in the late nineteenth century by Herman Hollerith at the urging of John Shaw Billings "for doing the purely mechanical work of

---

[83] Helen Shera showed me his tools, along with myriads of photographs and other memorabilia from Oxford, during a week of interviews with her in August 1983.
[84] Helen Shera, Interview by H. Curtis Wright, 23 August 1983.
[85] Ibid., adding that they also made a dog house together, and that they were very proud of it.
[86] Ibid.
[87] Jesse Shera, Interview by Mrs. Gerald R. Ruderman (1968), TMs, Archives, Case Western Reserve, Cleveland, Ohio.

tabulating population and similar statistics."[88] They were "predecessors of the IBMs,"[89] as Shera calls them, operating mechanically at first with perforated tapes (like player pianos), and then electrically at first with circuits through holes punched in insulated cards. The later models were equipped with mechanical feeding devices. Originally, however, you had to presort the cards yourself, punch holes in them by hand, and feed them manually to the machines; for only then would they count and sort the cards in various predetermined ways so you could make your tabulations.

Shera became thoroughly familiar with these machines through the recurring statistical problems of population research. "His interest in punched cards, tabulating machines, and the like, can be traced to the Scripps Foundation at Oxford," which also "leads to his aroused interest in mechanized information handling;"[90] for there it was that he first began to ponder the potential of machine applications to librarianship.

> [They were only] punched card sorters, really, counting or tabulating machines. But I began to think in a big sort of way, 'Gosh, why couldn't this kind of technique be used to prepare card catalogs, or to analyze the content of books? . . . Isn't there a possibility, somehow, to adapt these machines to the processing of information'? . . . I didn't know much about it, but I just kept on thinking about the thing. I thought it would be interesting to pursue it, but I didn't have any of the technical background . . . . I didn't know enough about the problem, I didn't know enough about the machines themselves, and all I could do was just kind of think about it.[91]

Early Experiments with Computing Machines

As a graduate student at Chicago, Shera "encountered ideas . . . that underscored and affirmed his own thinking" about the "philosophical, theoretical, and interdisciplinary approach to library

---

[88] *Dictionary of American Biography,* (New York: Charles Scribner's Sons, 1944) s.v. "Hollerith, Herman."
[89] Jesse Shera, Interview by Ruth Helmuth (1970), TMs, Archives, Case Western Reserve, Cleveland, Ohio.
[90] Helen Shera, Interview by author, 24 August 1983.
[91] Reconstructed from Shera's two accounts in the interviews by Ruderman and Helmuth (1968, 1970). The words are all his, but they jump back and forth between the two accounts.

service."[92] But little was said about the technology of communications. "We talked about it some there," he says, but "it never got beyond speculation."[93] He therefore tried to create interest in it.

> I began to talk to some of my fellow students, and even to some of the faculty, about this. Well, they got interested; but then I found out they were even less sophisticated than I was. They didn't know anything about computers either.[94]

In addition to that, he notes, "the University of Chicago has never had an engineering school. So, I never had anybody I could talk to at Chicago who might give me some help on this."[95]

At the OSS during the war, however, Shera began to experiment with an early IBM machine because one of the operations he supervised had to handle censorship intercepts, something for which conventional library methods had proved inadequate.

> These were pieces of mail from foreign countries that had to go through the U.S. Office of Censorship to be opened. And they sent this correspondence to us in these great masses of junk-- and a lot of it was junk. Nevertheless, our research staff was very much interested in it for the light it might throw on conditions in those countries.[96]

It was a small beginning. But Shera and his staff, drawing freely on his knowledge of tabulating machines and punched cards at the Scripps Foundation, began by "punching out this material, developing a standard list of subject headings (today we would call it a thesaurus) on IBM cards, and keying it to these letters taken by the Office of Censorship," in order to control an amorphous mass of documents. "It was all pretty crude," he recalled in 1968; "but here, in 1942, '43, and '44, we were playing with this kind of thing, and I was beginning to get some insight as to what could be done." It gave his own philosophy and thinking quite a boost, he adds, because "it was the first time I

---

[92] Margaret Kaltenback, "Shera, Jesse H.," in *ALA World Encyclopedia of Library and Information Services*, ed. R. Wedgeworth (Chicago: American Library Association, 1980), 525.
[93] Shera, Interview by Ruderman (1968).
[94] Shera, Interview by Helmuth (1970).
[95] Ibid.
[96] Ibid.

actually had a chance to experiment with this kind of thing in an actual operating situation."[97]

The involvement of machines with the informational and housekeeping functions of librarianship has now been growing steadily for at least half a century. "The basic idea of automated libraries was in the air" during the thirties and forties, although its early history has never been recorded.[98]

In 1939, Keppel was embarrassed to realize that librarians had watched "business machines juggle with payrolls and bankbooks" for many years before it ever occurred to them that those same machines "might be adapted to . . . library cards with equal dexterity." He predicted the appearance, within twenty years, or mechanized libraries, whose machines would render traditional catalogs and related bibliographic procedures obsolete because "the modern version of the old Hollerith machine will sort out and photograph anything the dial tells it, and . . . put all the cards back in their places."[99]

Tinkering with information machines was not uncommon in those days. "As early as 1935," for example, "Watson Davis had made sketches of a mechanized literature searching machine much like the Rapid Selector," which Ralph Shaw also designed at the time.[100] Soon after that, "the Minicard system was developed by Eastman Kodak."[101] These devices were all based on microfilm, which was derived from photography and combined with it to form the deep fascination of the thirties and forties with microphotography.[102]

As far back as 1876, Justin Winsor had been interested in the possibility of creating electrical and pneumatic machines "to facilitate delivery of books to branches of a public library."[103] At the University of Missouri in the late thirties, however, Ralph Parker was actually

---

[97] Shera, Interview by Ruderman (1968).
[98] Jesse H. Shera, "What's Past is Prologue: Beyond 1984," *ALA Bulletin* 62 (1967): 37. See also: Jesse H. Shera and Donald B. Cleveland, "History and Foundations of Information Science," *Annual Review of Information Science and Technology* 12 (1977): 254.
[99] Frederick J. Keppel, "Looking Forward," in *The Library of Tomorrow*, Emily Miller Danton, ed. (Chicago: American Library Association, 1939), 5. See also: Jesse H. Shera, "Documentation into Information Science," in *Strategies for Change in Information Programs*, William E. Hug, ed., (New York: Bowker, 1974): 275; Shera and Cleveland, 254; and Shera, "What's Past is Prologue," 35-36.
[100] Shera and Cleveland, 254.
[101] Ibid.
[102] Ibid, 254-54. See also: C. K. Schultz and P. L. Garwig, "History of the American Documentation Institute: a Sketch," *American Documentation* 20 (1969): 152-60.
[103] Jesse H. Shera, "Tomorrow, and Tomorrow, and Tomorrow," Review of *The Library of Tomorrow*, ed. Emily Danton, *ALA Bulletin* 33 (1939): 278, citing the chapter in *The Library of Tomorrow* written by Robert Downs.

experimenting with the mechanization of library housekeeping functions through the use of tabulating machines and similar equipment; and after that, automation began seeping into virtually every aspect of library operations.[104]

An important milestone was also reached in 1945, when an electrical engineer named Vannevar Bush combined the possibilities of microphotography and electronics in order to conjure up a computer-like device called "Memex," which "personalized the information retrieval machine . . . [and] caught the imagination of layman and professional alike."[105] It was something like an on-line computer: you could consult it with ease, and it contained all of the information anyone could possibly want.[106] It's potentialities were described by Bush at the close of World War II, when "the real computers were just beginning to be developed . . . . It was a kind of follow-up to Keppel's [prophetic] article in *The Library of Tomorrow*, and this started a lot of people to thinking."[107]

As a professor at the GLS from 1947 to 1952, Shera "pondered the implications of the new technology" from time to time.[108] He contacted Ralph Shaw, the Director of Libraries at the Department of Agriculture, who had already invented the rapid selector while working with Vannevar Bush.[109] Shaw "eventually built a rapid selector," says Shera, although he never really got it to function properly. "But we began to play around with this thing, and I [also] talked with other people."[110] One of those other people, he says, was "my old friend and former associate, Margaret Egan, who was no more sophisticated than I [was] in this computer business."[111]

> [She] was teaching a course in bibliographic organization and was very much interested in this thing. But she was social scientist . . . . and couldn't do any more about the actual engineering part of it than I could. Nevertheless, we were working together on this thing and talking about it and going to meetings.[112]

---

[104] Shera, "What's Past is Prologue," 37, 40-41.
[105] Shera, "Documentation into Information Science," 276.
[106] Shera, "What's Past is Prologue," 36.
[107] Shera, Interview by Ruderman (1968).
[108] Kaltenbach, "Shera, Jesse H.," 525.
[109] Theodore C. Hines, "Shaw and the Machine," in *Essays for Ralph Shaw*, Norman D. Stevens, ed., (Metuchen, N.J.: Scarecrow, 1975), 6.
[110] Shera, Interview by Helmuth (1970).
[111] Ibid.
[112] Ibid.

Meetings, Conferences, and Breakthroughs

Shera and Egan also sponsored their own meeting, the Fifteenth Annual Conference of the GLS in July, 1950, where the problems of bibliographic organization were discussed and "Ralph Shaw described for the first time the theory underlying the Rapid Selector."[113] Then, less than two years later, a couple of things happened that helped complete the stage setting for the birth of information science in the fifties.

First, Shera met James W. Perry, a chemist at MIT who had been funded by the Carnegie Corporation to work on a project called "Scientific Aids to Learning," which was set up "to deal with the automation and mechanization of the resources of scholarship."[114] In the Spring of 1952, Perry organized a conference at MIT "on the application of machines to scientific information," where Jess met him and his associates for the first time.[115] This conference "was really a review of what they were doing," Shera recalls, "and he invited me to come to it. So, I went. And there, I met everybody who was anybody at all in this field. They were *all* there, "all of the people who were working with information problems and machines.[116]

> It was there that I first saw one of the 'giant brains,' as they called them in those days. It was the machine MIT built . . . called 'Whirlwind.' It was one of the first, and perhaps *the* first of the big computers. They had a whole room full of shelving filled with electronic tubes and capacitors and resistors, and just shelf after shelf of this stuff. It was a huge business. I remember going through it with Ralph Shaw, and Ralph said, 'I wonder what would happen if I loosened just one connection in all this mess of gear?'[117]

This conference was pivotal in shaping Shera's understanding of librarianship and information science. He was "terribly excited about it" when he discussed its significance with Margaret Egan after returning to Chicago,[118] for "James W. Perry . . . was among the foremost of the pioneers" in the information movement: "his studies in machine literature searching laid the intellectual, and to some extent the

---

[113] Shera and Cleveland, 255.
[114] Shera, Interview by Ruderman (1968).
[115] Ibid.; and Shera, "What's Past is Prologue," 37.
[116] Shera, Interview by Helmuth (1970).
[117] Ibid.
[118] Ibid.

technological, foundations of information retrieval as they are largely understood today"[119]

Reorganizing the American Documentation Institute

The second thing Shera did was "to participate incisively in . . . [reorganizing] the American Documentation Institute . . . early in 1952." [120] The institute's new journal, *American Documentation*, was launched in January, 1950, under a grant from the Carnegie Corporation by Vernon D. Tate, an editor with strong conservative interests in microphotography who was also the "immediate past president of ADI."[121] On February 1950, however, the Librarian of Congress, Luther Evans, succeeded Tate as president of the ADI, which was subsequently relocated in Washington, D. C. Evans, unlike Tate, was progressive in outlook, an internationalist who reorganized the ADI along democratic lines and opened its membership to anyone interested in the technology of communications. After two years, when his grant ran out, Tate was also replaced as editor by Mortimer Taube, a progressive thinker whose views were compatible with Evans. "The transfer of . . . editorship from Tate to Taube was significant" because it marked an important change in the ADI. "Taube's editorship and Evan's presidency . . . directed the institute away from microphotography" and turned it towards alternative forms of communications technology.[122]

These new interests triggered the rise of electronics and the decline of microfilm in the ADI, a trend which grew progressively stronger until "finally, the influence of the microphotographers . . . waned" so badly that they withdrew from the institute and "formed the National Microfilm Association."[123]

The ADI, reviving from the gradual decay it had experienced since the thirties, was now headquartered at the Library of Congress. It was being restructured from the ground up, for it was breaking with its old traditions and attracting "a lot of these queer nonlibrary types," the electronic freaks "who were playing around with this information problem."[124]

---

[119] Shera, "What's Past is Prologue," 37.
[120] *The Encyclopedia of Library and Information Science*, Volume 38 (New York: Marcel Dekker, 1985). S.v. "Shera, Jesse Hauk" by C. H. Rawski.
[121] Schultz and Garwig, 156.
[122] Shera and Cleveland, 255-56.
[123] Ibid., 256.
[124] Shera, Interview by Ruderman (1968).

Shera was "one of the charter members of the ADI after it was revived," as were Evans, Perry, Taube, and others. These charter members now became actively involved with each other in addressing the information problem: they formed a group, which included Shera and Perry, "and began to do a lot of talking."[125] Shera's interaction with "these queer nonlibrary types" in Cambridge, Massachusetts, and Washington D. C. was shortly to have a profound impact on the library profession. "But," he tells us, "all I did at Chicago really, was to think about these things and talk about them. And not being an engineer myself, or a mathematician, I couldn't do much constructively."[126]

---

[125] Ibid.
[126] Ibid.

CHAPTER 3
BRIDGING THE GAP AT WESTERN RESERVE

Shera's Appointment

In the Spring of 1952, while Shera was pondering the possibilities of automated library procedures and mechanized literature searching, John Schoff Millis, President of Western Reserve University, was instituting some badly needed reforms in professional education. Millis wanted, among other things, a new dean for his library school, because, he says, "the same kind of educational revolution was required there that was [already] occurring in the medical school, and being talked about in nursing and in social work. There hadn't been a good shake-up of education in the history of the field,"[127] he adds, and he clearly meant to shake things up but good.

The library school was not alone in this, of course, for Millis apparently wanted all of the professional schools to clean up their academic acts by dealing with their rampant vocationalism and lining up with the rest of the university. But the current dean of the library school, Miss Thirza Grant, was thoroughly traditional and nonacademic in her educational outlook. She felt, accordingly, "that Millis didn't have any real confidence in her;"[128] and she was absolutely right: "he felt that she was a nice motherly soul, and Millis wasn't interested in motherly souls."[129] He was interested in finding a dean who knew the functions and purposes of the library profession and wanted to create an appropriate graduate education to go with them.[130]

---

[127] John S. Millis, Interview by W. K. Cawley, 27 June 1983. Tape recorded transcript, Archives, Case Western University, Cleveland, Ohio.
[128] Jesse Shera, Interview by Ruth Helmuth, 1970. A copy of the interview is available in the Case Western Reserve Archives, Cleveland, Ohio. Shera is here drawing on information about Miss Grant from Margaret Kaltenbach, Miss Grant's long-time confidante and close associate.
[129] Ibid. Shera also adds: "I'm sure Millis didn't have any confidence in her, although he's never said anything--except little snide remarks about the library school before I came, . . . remarks like 'I knew there was something to this library education business . . . ,' remarks like that. And also what Peg [Kaltenbach] said about Miss Grant," ibid.
[130] Miss Grant was a capable, conscientious, old-line traditionalist who was just not up to coping with the kind of academic rigor demanded by Millis. Shera hardly knew her, and yet he speaks of her with the kind of fond affection we all feel for the "Miss Grants" we have known. "She never left Cleveland. She never participated in the state library association or in ALA. She just stayed here [at Reserve] and tended her little garden. It was a well-tended little garden . . . . I'll have to say this for Miss Grant: she

In the early summer of 1952, Shera yielded to the urgings of Pierce Butler and Margaret Egan and applied for the deanship at Reserve. He was reluctant to apply at first, because Millis had rejected him for the position of University Librarian at the University of Vermont in 1956.[131] But Shera didn't know that Millis had rejected him because "he was a very remarkable person, much too good for the job of university librarian."[132]

Millis had contacted Ralph Beals, Director of Libraries at the University of Chicago, about possible candidates for that position, and Beals had told him about Shera. "I have tossed his name in with the rest," he said, "but I don't want him to go, and I'm going to do everything I can to keep him at Chicago. Nevertheless, I think he ought to have the chance."[133] Millis respected that, apparently. "But I made a very substantial notation," he says, "as I always did when I met somebody I would like to employ in the future. So, when the deanship of the library school came open here [at Reserve], I already had my candidate."[134]

Shera, therefore, did not get the polite rejection not the expected from President Millis. "Much to my astonishment," he says, "I got back in an incredibly short time [a positive response]: 'Yes, I remember you very well and we'd like very much to talk to you. How soon can you come to Cleveland?'"[135] The deanship was appealing for several reasons. The financial condition of the GLS was deplorable, for example, and its academic condition, if anything, was even worse.[136] "And also," Shera

---

certainly attracted the loyalty of the students, the old-timers. And apparently her course in book selection, which was her great course, really was a marvelous course--I've heard that from too many people for it to be wrong. And certainly, she developed a substantial body of devoted alumni. So, as I say, it was a well-tended garden. All I needed to do was to start in and go on from there. And with the support I got from the administration it was pretty hard to fail," ibid.

[131] Shera discusses this at some length in the interviews by Ruderman (Jesse Shera, Interview by Mrs. Gerald H. Ruderman, 1968. Copy available in the Case Western Reserve Archives, Cleveland, Ohio) and Helmuth, 1970.

[132] Millis, Interview by Cawley, 27 June 1983.

[133] Paraphrase of Beals' words to Shera: "I don't want you to go, but I tossed your name in, and I told Millis at the same time I'd do everything I could to keep you here. But nevertheless, I thought you ought to have a chance," Jesse Shera, Interview by Helmuth (1970).

[134] Millis, Interview by Cawley, 27 June 1983, adding that "I had added a bit to my record of him, having seen several things that he'd written in journals which tickled me a good deal."

[135] Shera, Interview by Ruderman (1968). The last sentence of this quotation comes from the parallel account in the Interview by Helmuth (1970).

[136] "As to why I came, there are several reasons. One was that the University of

tells us, "I was intrigued by the idea of running my own school and doing some of the things I wanted to do."[137]

> One of the reasons I wanted to go, and one of the reasons Margaret Egan wanted me to go, was that here was a chance. She and I had both tried terribly hard at Chicago to get them interested in this whole field of documentation, automation, and machines . . . . And Margaret said, 'This is a chance for you to go to Western Reserve and run your own school and develop something on this line.' And this was one of the things I wanted to talk to Millis about.[138]

The concerns of President Millis became apparent when the interviews began. "I definitely had the feeling," says Shera, "that he was unhappy with the library school." Its faculty was solid: "they were all good people, all competent people; but it was terribly small and very traditionally oriented," and the feeling persisted that "Jack was saying to himself, 'let's either do something with this school . . . or get rid of it, one way or the other.'" It may not have been that drastic, Shera notes, "but I had the feeling that he felt something had to be done about the school."[139] And that set the tone for the rest of the interviews.

A New Vision of Librarianship

> The thing I pounded on most, particularly with Jack Millis, was the possibility of creating a new kind of librarianship . . . . So, I talked, not only about library education, but about the whole problem with automation and computers, and about the tremendous opportunity [this was] for exploring some of these new developments and what they might mean for a new type of librarianship.[140]

Millis was fascinated with the prospect of creating a new librarianship, says Shera, "and we had some very good discussions."[141] Millis was also pleased with Shera's understanding of librarianship.

Chicago . . . was in a terrible financial state . . . . So, there were no promotions in Chicago . . . . [Another] was that I'd been increasingly dissatisfied with the way things were going [at the GLS]," ibid.
[137] Ibid.
[138] Shera, Interview by Ruderman (1968).
[139] Shera, Interview by Helmuth (1970).
[140] Ibid.
[141] Ibid.

"Nobody had really thought about it as a profession," he says; "it was thought of as a technique, a calling. Jesse Shera was the first person in my acquaintance who though as I did, namely, that if librarianship was to be a profession, it would require a different kind of educational program than the one it had at Reserve--it would require a program with exacting standards, rigorous expectations, a competent faculty, basic research, and fundamental scholarship.[142] In short, Shera informs us, the response of President Millis to these interviews was succinct and positive. "He said, 'This sounds interesting . . . .' I said, 'Well, that's the direction I want to develop.' And the upshot was that I came" to Cleveland.[143]

John Schoff Millis had an unacknowledged importance in American librarianship. If he had not been a tough-minded university president who wanted his library school to justify its presence in an academic institution, and if he had not recognized the worth of Jesse Hauk Shera, none of the things that happened after Shera came to Cleveland would have happened at all.

Those interviews marked the beginning of a beautiful friendship, for Shera and Millis had common interests from the outset and have been close ever since. "He permeates the whole situation," says Shera. "He supported me in the same way Ralph [Beals] did" at Chicago. "There's never going to be another Jack Millis . . . . I was his man for the job, and it's never going to be like that again."[144] This deanship, certainly, is "one of the most fruitful and felicitous of appointments" in library history.[145] Jack! Gosh, what I owe to Jack!" says Shera.[146] And the library profession might also ponder what it owes to Jack.

The librarianship envisioned by Shera in 1952, which was still a newborn babe wrapped in the swaddling clothes of microphotography, was struggling to become the lusty infant of information science. The new ADI, shorn of its old conservatism, had broken with the microfilm enthusiasts and was beginning to think seriously about automating the

---

[142] Millis, Interview by Cawley, 27 June 1983. "One of the promises I got out of Millis was that we could build a larger full-time faculty. I said, 'It's just too small a faculty.' And he agreed to this," Shera, Interview by Ruderman (1968).
[143] Ibid.
[144] Shera, Interview by Helmuth (1970), adding that "If the University of Chicago had done for the GLS what Jack had done for me, it would have been a different story at Chicago!"
[145] Margaret Kaltenbach, "Shera, Jesse H.," in *ALA World Encyclopedia of Library and Information Science*, ed. R. Wedgeworth (Chicago: American Library Association, 1980), 525.
[146] Shera, Interview by Helmuth (1970).

routines and procedures of librarianship and mechanizing the retrieval of information from documents.

The early fifties were optimistic days of "unlimited promise, high hopes, and unrestrained enthusiasm," in which the realization of push-button libraries through machine applications seemed just around the corner.[147] There were great expectations, as documentalists watched each new development in such things as minicards, paper tape, punched cards, notched cards, magnetic tape, coordinate indexing, and zatocoding. "To all of these battles on the fringes of the library world, the conventional librarians remained relatively indifferent."[148] The American Library Association, sleeping furiously as usual, "was more concerned with its organizational structure than with technological innovation at its margins."[149]

An unfortunate breach was opening between librarianship and documentation: the wheel was constantly being reinvented by the documentalists, who thus triggered an obstinate controversy between librarians and the information troops, which has long since become boring and unproductive because, for all the changes in traditional library procedures, "there has never been . . . any evidence to show that the practices concerned were genuinely new, and not merely improvements."[150]

Gradually, and perhaps perforce, the librarians began "looking at their operations from a refreshingly new point of view," although they recommitted the cardinal sin of American librarianship--the Deweyite failure to distinguish the physics of library operations from the metaphysics of librarianship, in which the librarian's end becomes an understanding of the means and librarianship degenerates into a means without ends--by focusing on the machine itself before they had formed a clear and unambiguous concept of what the machine should be the means of accomplishing.[151]

But it was not until the early sixties, really, that librarians paid "any substantial degree of attention to what was taking place," and even then they were mostly interested in automating their housekeeping

---

[147] Jesse H. Shera, "Documentation into Computer Science," in *Strategies for Change in Information Programs*, Williams E. Hug, ed. (New York: Bowker, 1974), 275.
[148] Ibid. 276.
[149] Ibid.
[150] D. J. Foskett, "Progress in Documentation," *Journal of Documentation* 26 (1970): 343.
[151] Shera, "Documentation into Computer Science," 276. I have discussed the original sin of American librarianship and related matters in "The Substance of Librarianship," *Utah Libraries* 19 (Spring 1976): 27-33.

functions."[152] It is not surprising that the automation of empirical procedures was successful and mechanized information retrieval was not, for here too, the former is the means of doing a job whereas the latter is the job that needs doing.[153]

Center for Documentation and Communication Research Founded

In November, 1952, less than three months after Shera came to Cleveland, he learned that Allen Kent and James W. Perry, whose Carnegie grant had run out, were leaving MIT for the Battelle Memorial Institute (BMI) in Columbus. This move made neighbors of Shera and Perry, who therefore decided to get together as often as they could and work on the retrieval problem. "We did see each other quite frequently," says Shera, whenever "he'd come through Cleveland or I'd have something to take me to Columbus."[154]

While Perry was at Battelle, moreover, Shera arranged "the transfer in 1953 of the editorial and business offices of *American Documentation*, the official journal of the American Documentation Institute, from Washington D. C., to the SLS at Western Reserve,[155] a move which accomplished three things: (1) it "enhanced the prestige of the institution [WRU];" (2) it "contributed to the [library] school's growing national reputation;" and (3) it "laid the ground-work for the establishment of the Center for Documentation and Communication Research (CDCR)" in 1955, which was to become "a prime example of educational experimentation involving basic and applied research in . . . information retrieval."[156] During this period, Perry and his staff also asked for Shera's help in planning an international conference to be sponsored jointly by WRU and BMI on the uses of recorded knowledge.[157]

In 1954, however, things started falling apart at Battelle. Clyde Williams, the President of BMI who had hired Perry, was up for

---

[152] Shera, "Documentation into Computer Science," 278.
[153] Ibid.
[154] Shera, Interview by Helmuth (1970). See also the parallel account in the Ruderman Interview (1968).
[155] *The Encyclopedia of Library and Information Science*. Volume 38 (New York: Marcel Dekker, 1985), s.v. "Shera, Jesse Hauk" by C. H. Rawski.
[156] Ibid. citing C. H. Cramer, *The School of Library Science at Case Western Reserve University, 1904-1979* (Cleveland, Ohio: Case Western University, 1979), 91.
[157] Kaltenbach, "Shera, Jesse H.," 525. See the Shera Interview by Ruderman (1968) for details.

retirement; and his prospective replacements were all new Pharaohs who knew not Joseph and couldn't have cared less about the information problem.[158] In the spring of 1955, therefore, Perry came to Cleveland and told Shera it was all over at Columbus. It happened "on a Saturday," says Shera. "I remember it very well."[159]

> We had lunch at the Brick Cottage. . . . And I said, 'You know, Jim, this really belongs in a library school, because this is librarianship, darn it, and you ought to be connected with a library school. Why don't we explore the possibility of your coming up here? Maybe we can set up a center to work in this area.' Well, this made a lot of sense [to him], and he said, 'I hadn't really thought of it this way, but I get your point.' And I said, 'let me talk to President Millis and see how he reacts to this and I'll be in touch with you.' The next week, then, I talked to President Millis, and he caught fire immediately on this thing.[160]

Millis said to Shera, "I always knew there was something to librarianship; I didn't know quite what it was, but I am beginning to see it. . . . Tell Perry to come up, and we'll talk to him."[161] So Perry came to Cleveland with his associate, Allen Kent, for interviews with Millis. "Before I knew it," says Shera, "I had Perry and Kent on my faculty and a documentation center on my hands."[162]

The documentation center was established late in the Spring of 1955 by Millis and Shera as a research division of the library school, with Perry as Director and Kent as Associate Director.[163] "In the Fall of 1955," Shera tells us, "I brought Margaret Egan [to Reserve] from Chicago, and we really thought we were going to get down to things."[164] And they did--sort of. By 1956, Shera's coterie of enthusiasts, "all concerned with . . . documentation and machine literature searching," were committed to the task of "establishing a new look in librarianship" at Reserve.[165]

---

[158] Shera, Interview by Helmuth (1970).
[159] Ibid.
[160] Shera, Interview by Ruderman (1968).
[161] The first sentence is from the Shera Interview by Helmuth (1970), the second from the Shera Interview by Ruderman (1968).
[162] Shera, Interview by Helmuth (1970).
[163] Ibid, where Shera says it "was set up about May of 1955."
[164] Ibid.
[165] Alan M. Rees, "Jesse H. Shera: a Reminiscence," *Information* 3 (March-April, 1971): 105.

Shera, who describes himself as "pretty machine oriented in those days,"[166] was thoroughly convinced that machine methods would enhance librarianship "and extend the professional competence of the librarian."[167] The American Society for Metals had given the documentation center a grant of $75,000 for "research on the application of machine methods to organize and abstract the literature of metallurgy,"[168] and Perry was hard at work building his searching selector in Shera's basement.[169] "It was an elaborate system of electric relays" and untold miles of wire "activated by punched paper tape," and it made an awful noise; but the thing actually worked: "it worked very well for several years," as a matter of fact, while "its gargantuan size and resplendent flashing lights impressed adults and frightened children."[170]

Perry also managed to get General Electric interested in what he was doing, and its engineers then "devised the GE 225 general-purpose computer," which could be adapted to the kind of literature searching the center was interested in, and "made the first one available at nominal cost to the library school."[171] Thus it was the first operational system for the mechanized retrieval of information, the first operational computer, showed up in the library school at Western Reserve University,[172] which also became "the first library school to . . . [incorporate] documentation into tis academic program."[173]

The initial grant of the American Society for Metals, which led to the center's original successes, then helped to attract "many more [grants] from a wide variety of governmental and corporate sources."[174] These grants were paralleled by "a series of national and international conferences, skillfully organized after the model of Shera's practice at

---

[166] Shera, Interview by Helmuth (1970).
[167] Rees, "Jesse H. Shera," 106.
[168] Cramer, 95.
[169] Rees, "Jesse H. Shera," 107.
[170] Cramer, 93.
[171] Ibid. Shera notes that this computer was still in use in 1968 (Shera, Interviewed by Ruderman).
[172] Alan M. Rees, Interview by H. Curtis Wright, 26 August 1983. "Western Reserve University was strong in the natural and medical sciences, but ironically the first computers in a professional school on its campus were in the School of Library Science," Cramer, 93.
[173] Rees, "Jesse H. Shera," 105.
[174] Cramer, 95, adding that those sources included "the National Institutes of Health, the National Science Foundation, the American Diabetic Association, Union carbide, the H. W. Wilson Company, the U.S. Air Force Office of Scientific research, the U.S. Office of Education, the American Chemical Society, and the Special Libraries Association."

Chicago's GLS."[175] In 1956, the conference planned by Perry and Shera on the "Practical Utilization of Recorded Knowledge (PURK) was attended by "700 librarians, administrators, and research directors." It was a unique conference because, for the first time ever, "librarians were discussing the organization of recorded information with representatives from business, industry, and . . . government."[176]

In 1957, a conference on "Systems for Information Retrieval" attracted 900 specialists.[177] In 1959, a week-long international conference was sponsored jointly with the Rand Development Corporation on standards of a common language for machine searching and translation. This conference "brought to University Circle 200 representatives from fifteen nations in all parts of the world, including iron-curtain [nations]," and created an atmosphere at Reserve "not unlike that in the United Nations or [in] a university . . . [with] an international studentbody."[178]

Finally, says Shera, "I began to feel . . . [a bit] conference happy. . . . Other people were beginning to hold conferences [by then] . . . , so I said, 'Let's rest on our oars for a while."[179] Yet these conferences "were very important contributions, really,"[180] because they "called attention to the information explosion" in the fifties and "provided a platform for . . . public debate on the nature and extent of the information crisis" by bringing together "managers of the major abstracting and indexing services, personnel from government agencies, congressmen, and representatives from industry."[181]

Fundamental problems were thus explored by the Western Reserve group, who emphasized the need for creating information agencies like the National Referral Center for Science and Technology and the Science Information Exchange.[182] This group also seized every opportunity to publicize the ominous implications of Sputnik in 1957 by stressing the importance of scholarly communications in general and dramatizing the deficiencies of scientific communication "in the United States" as compared with "colossal Russian efforts" in these matters.

---

[175] Rawski. Cf. Cramer, 96: "One of the methods utilized by the University of Chicago to disseminate knowledge was the conference; Shera adopted the same system on a national and international basis."
[176] Ibid.
[177] Ibid.
[178] Ibid.
[179] Shera, Interview by Ruderman (1968).
[180] Ibid.
[181] Rees, "Jesse H. Shera," 106.
[182] Ibid.

It was cogently argued that national security was at stake. Shera, Perry and Kent presented testimony before congressional hearings conducted by . . . Senator [Hubert H.] Humphrey, calling for increased U.S. effort in the organization and dissemination of scientific and technical information.[183]

All of the above contributed mightily to the intensely intellectual climate in Shera's School of Library Science and brought him national and international recognition. He had "initiated an era of fame and renown" exceeding anything Reserve had ever known,[184] and the sixties were barely launched before he "was firmly established world-wide as one of the grand old men of the information field."[185] The electrifying climate in Shera's challenging new world of information retrieval on an international scale has been described as "elevated and inspiring" by Alan Rees, an unsuspecting student from Ohio State who arrived at Reserve in 1956 to go through library school.[186]

> Expecting conventional training in library techniques, I discovered [instead] an environment reflecting great intellectual vigor, excitement and . . . arrogance. Perry and Kent labored in [the Documentation Center on Magnolia Drive] . . . while the Library School was located in the Freiberger Library [on Bellflower Road]. Trudging between these [two organizations] . . . made me wonder as to the relationship between [them]--which was the tail and which was the dog . . . .
>
> And so I was plunged into the Shera-Perry-Kent documentation arena. Through them I gained an *entree* to the [newly discovered] world of [information retrieval] . . . . The atmosphere was exciting and invigorating with much argument to the point of rudeness and insult. There was great expectation

---

[183] Ibid. "One could well argue that . . . Sputnik . . . revived the ADI. This Russian achievement . . . pushed information needs to the forefront in the scientific community. Senator Hubert Humphrey . . . held a series of hearings designed to push the National Science Foundation into increased support for research into . . . the organization and retrieval of scientific information," Jesse H. Shera and Donald B. Cleveland, "History and Foundations of information Science," *Annual Review of Information Science and Technology* 12 (1977): 257. See also U.S. Congress, Subcommittee of the Committee on Government Operations, 1958. *Hearings on the Science and Technology Act of 1958* (Washington D. C.: Government Printing Office, 1958).
[184] Margaret Kaltenbach, "Biography of Jesse Shera," TMs, Archives, Case Western Reserve University, Cleveland, Ohio.
[185] Rawski.
[186] Rees, Interview by Wright, 26 August 1983.

and the prevailing feeling nationally was one of imminent discovery and concern with prior claims and intellectual authorship.[187]

Disintegration of the Center

There were, perhaps, no serpents in Shera's garden. However, arrogance, argument, rudeness and insult, concern with prior claims and intellectual authorship--these products of noxious weeds were indeed found among the fruits of his successes. It wasn't easy to stay ahead of the weeds. There were some awful setbacks, to be sure, and one of them was the death of Margaret Egan in January, 1959. "That just shocked things," Shera tells us, "because we had worked very closely on this" both in Chicago and at Reserve.[188] "God, I remember the day she died," he says. "I felt as if half of me had gone! How could I go on without this gal?"[189]

Still, he did go on, although her death was one of those losses he never recovered from.[190] He went on in spite of another setback, his intellectual battles with James Perry and Allen Kent. The documentation center was begotten by Shera and born of the library school; but the child soon grew stronger than its parents, threatening to leave home at an early age, and Shera began his prolonged struggle to keep the family together. "He was convinced that if librarianship was to survive as a profession it had to rise above the computer, the systems analyst, and the engineer. At the same time," however, "he did not believe that technological innovations had to be disruptive."[191] He believed, to the contrary, that the powerful instruments of modern technology should be used by librarians to create whole new dimensions of library service.

The CDCR was originally based on the idea, shared in common by Millis and Shera, that "the center should be what Jack called a

---

[187] Rees, "Jesse H. Shera," 106.
[188] Shera, Interview by Helmuth (1970),adding that "She was a brilliant gal, really, almost a genius in some ways. I owe her a tremendous debt because her influence on my thinking is probably greater than that of any other person: certainly it's greater than anybody else's about library problems--there's no question about that."
[189] Ibid. When Rees met Shera and his staff in 1956, he characterized all of them as brilliant people; but he pointed to Margaret Egan, who "pushed philosophy like mad," as "especially brilliant--even more so than Shera," Rees, Interview by H. Curtis Wright, 26 August 1983.
[190] Paraphrasing Helmuth's remark, verified by Shera, that Egan's death was "one of those losses you never recover from," Shera, Interview by Helmuth (1970).
[191] Cramer, 99.

catalyst,"[192] an integrating agent whose function was to galvanize the growing mass of splintered and unrelated attempts at automation and mechanized literature searching into an interlocked synthetic unity of some sort in which everything could be examined within the context of its interactions with everything else. Shera was betting on fusion, in other words. But what he got was fission, because Kent and Perry "had their own ideas," as Millis puts it.[193] Shera intended to set the center up as an adjunct to the library school, "a research unit that would examine all these . . . [information devices] as objectively as we could, and try to get some fundamental research done."[194] The idea of a high-tech synthesis "never really took,[195] therefore, because "Perry had developed his own system, and he was all hell-bent for that and didn't want to work on anything else. And actually, he never did."[196] Perry's system "was a good system,"[197] says Shera.

> I mean, we learned an awful lot in working with that thing. But all the attention of [Perry and his staff] . . . was focused on this particular system, which came to be known, much to my unhappiness, really, as *the* Western Reserve System. And I didn't like it. . . . Whatever synthesis we had was simply measuring everything else against what Perry had done, and it was [always] inferior, according to Perry.[198]

Conflicts like this, which ultimately led to Perry's resignation from Western Reserve University, also let Perry and Shera to regard each other as somewhat narrow-minded. "My best accomplishments are the direct result of interest in diverse fields," Perry told President Millis in an unsuccessful attempt to out-maneuver Shera. "The field of research in which I would like to work is far broader than documentation or library science." This, he was quick to add, is one of the major reasons "for requesting that my appointment be so formulated as to place me outside the School of Library Science."[199]

Most of Perry's "diverse fields," however, were subdivisions of engineering, whereas Shera tended to view engineering itself as overly preoccupied with the technical aspect of everything. "I've got a lot of

---

[192] Shera, Interview by Helmuth (1970).
[193] Millis, Interview by Cawley, 27 June 1983.
[194] Shera, Interview by Helmuth (1970).
[195] Shera, Interview by Ruderman (1968).
[196] Shera, Interview by Helmuth (1970).
[197] Shera, Interview by Ruderman (1968).
[198] Ibid., Italics his.
[199] James W. Perry to John S. Millis, March 29, 1960.

respect for engineers," he says. "They can do marvelous things; but Lord, they're awful narrow. . . . I do wish they were broader in their interests."[200] When the engineers charge that librarians are innumerate, furthermore, they lay themselves wide open to the counter charge of illiteracy: it is a well-known fact that they have used the library less, and thus approached more closely to illiteracy, than anyone else in the academic community. English, as Shera was fond of saying, is a foreign language to the engineers, whose *Muttersprache* is mathematics. But Perry didn't wholly fit this caricature. For all of their differences in these and other respects, Shera always acknowledged Perry as a kind of erratic but authentic genius. His mathematical and linguistic insights into the myriad problems of information retrieval were truly outstanding, according to Shera, and "the whole field owes a tremendous debt to him."[201]

> I don't regret what Perry did, even though it wasn't exactly what I wanted, because he . . . [showed] the complexity of these problems of information searching--the problems of linguistics, of language, and even of sentence structure and the analyzing of questions. He made a very important contribution . . . that really should be recognized, even though he did spend a lot of time working on his own stuff . . . He showed that . . . [information] problems were complicated and were not going to be solved by simple kinds of *ad hoc* methods. So I don't have any regrets about it all, but I do wish we could have started earlier on actual analysis of other types of mechanisms.[202]

Lessons Learned

Many have noted that "Shera showed great foresight in establishing a Center for Documentation in the School of Library Science and that this was a major contribution to library education."[203] Fewer realize, perhaps, that he also saw this as a perilous venture with a marvelous potential for tomfoolery and nonsense.[204] On February 23, 1961, not long after Perry left Reserve for the University of Arizona, Shera made the following public statement.

---

[200] Shera, Interview by Ruderman (1968).
[201] Ibid.
[202] Shera, Interview by Helmuth (1970).
[203] Rees, "Jesse H. Shera," 106.
[204] "He foresaw some dangers here, and also saw them realized," Helen Shera, Interview by H. Curtis Wright, 25 August, 1983.

> The mechanization of information storage and retrieval has much to contribute to the [real] solution of the library problem, but with it comes the danger of . . . over-simplified solutions and . . . panaceas. The over-selling of an idea . . . in its experimental stages will [inevitably] lead to sketchy and ill-defined programs, the prostitution of ideals, and a sacrifice of quality. . . . Because a particular literature searching device may . . . work well in a . . . circumscribed pilot operation, the undiscriminating may see in it the solution to all bibliographic problems, and a tentative proposal may become a fad. . . . The relationship between reader and book, between literature searched and literature searcher, is far more complex and subtle than has been supposed. . . . We do not pretend to have solved the information retrieval problem at Western Reserve. But if we have learned anything from our investigations it is that one cannot begin with hardware, with a machine, and work backward to the solution of the problem.[205]

This statement illuminates the complex struggles involving (1) academic altruism and opportunism, (2) professional altruism, and (3) commercial opportunism which occurred at Reserve between 1955 and 1963. The resulting conflict of outlooks may be analyzed as follows:

1. <u>The academic outlook</u> is the intellectual spirit of serious critical inquiry found in competent university professors the world over. It may be humanistic, scientific, or both; it may be altruistic (if it benefits the university as well as the professor) or opportunistic (if it benefits only the professor); and it may or may not include commitment to a specific profession or group of professions.

2. <u>The professional outlook</u> is essentially the academic outlook tempered by an altruistic commitment to the special interests of a specific profession or group of professions.

3. <u>The commercial outlook</u> subordinates academic and professional values (and in its radical forms all values) to the marketing ethic of the salesman, whose operating principle is the maximization of profits. It is predominantly (or wholly) opportunistic: the idea is to buy (or produce) something for as little as possible and sell it for as much as possible.

---

[205] Jesse H. Shera, "Development in machine Literature Searching," in his *Documentation and Organization of Knowledge*, D. J. Foskett, ed., (Hamden, Conn.: Archon Books, 1966), 105-6.

Shera's interest in the documentation center was essentially professional: his outlook was academic in a fundamentally humanistic sense, and he was thoroughly committed to the improvement of librarianship. He therefore took the user's view of the Searching Selector as an object of scrutiny, not the subjective view assumed by its inventor, and looked at Perry' system (as he looked at all information systems) in terms of (1) the functions it could actually perform and (2) the purposes it might be able to serve by performing its functions; and he evaluated the system by its ability (or inability) to perform the functions and serve the purposes of librarianship.

This view, however, seemed restrictive and confining to Perry, "an extremely imaginative person" whose inventive mind was continually combining innovative and original ideas with "a very keen perception of the information problem."[206] Perry, too, was academically minded, but in an almost wholly scientific sense; and like most professors who lack Shera's strong commitment to a profession, he tended to view what he was doing in terms of his own career.

This led Shera to observe that self-interested scholars like Bliss, Ranganathan, and Perry, for whom objectivity means criticizing everybody *else's* assumptions, are very proficient when it comes to evaluating other people's systems. "When they develop systems of their own," however, "they just sell their souls to the devil;" and "the minute they start talking about the systems they've devised themselves, they lose their objectivity and are just as blind as anybody else to the weaknesses in their own systems."[207]

Nevertheless, says Shera, "Perry made an enormous contribution" to librarianship which must be acknowledged by the profession.[208] He was the foremost contender of the fifties, when documentalists everywhere, driven by the seductive prospect of imminent success, were striving frantically to resolve the problems of mechanized literature searching. "There was cutthroat competition in the field," Shera recalls, "and Perry was right in the thick of it."[209] He was probably not averse to profiting financially from his inventions, although his priorities were so overwhelmingly intellectual that money was virtually excluded from his preoccupations. The promotion of Perry's system was therefore left to Kent, the pragmatic and aggressive Associate Director of the Documentation Center.

---

[206] Shera, Interview by Ruderman (1968).
[207] Ibid.
[208] Ibid.
[209] Shera, Interview by Helmuth (1970).

His commercial ambitions, however, were constantly threatened by Shera, who saw the wealth, the prestige, and the tremendous success of the center "as a shot in the arm for librarianship."[210] But Perry and Kent, and particularly Kent, dissented from this, each for his own reasons, and a split developed between the center and the school in which Shera polarized "first with Kent, and then to some extent with Perry."[211] Both Kent and Perry "were convinced that they held the answer to the literature problem" and determined to exploit it, albeit in different ways.[212] The Western Reserve University system "was [accordingly] pronounced a success" and "offered . . . to subscribers" without an "extensive evaluation of . . . [its] complex intellectual apparatus."[213]

This scandalized Shera, who "was concerned with the intellectual foundations of machine systems" generally, whereas "Perry and Kent were intent on advancing, justifying and selling *their* system."[214] He was annoyed when they "exerted pressure on the National Science Foundation" through such things as congressional hearings and the Sputnik hysteria; he was apprehensive about the "national and international prominence" which "brought grants, influence and power to the center," but also "produced much tension in the university;" and he bristled when they "got investors from powerful financial interests" and threatened to "spin off" from the library school.[215]

He came to see them as dissenters who wanted to break with their parent organization and establish the documentation center as a separate institute independent of both the library school and the university. Thus, the original purpose of the center, which was essentially altruistic and professional in character, was being sacrificed to personal concerns of an academic and commercial nature, "and the library school began to fall apart."[216]

---

[210] Rees, Interview by H. Curtis Wright, 26 August 1983.
[211] Ibid.
[212] Rees, "Jesse H. Shera," 107.
[213] Ibid., adding that there was only "a limited test of the performance of the WRU Systems . . . by Cyril Cleverdon in 1962." See Association of Special Libraries and Information Bureaux, Cranfield Research Project, *A Report on a Test of the Index of Metallurgical Literature of Western Reserve University*, by Jean Aitchison and Cyril Cleverdon (Cranfield, Eng: College of Aeronautics, 1963), passim.
[214] Ibid., Rees, "Jesse H. Shera," 107.
[215] Ibid.
[216] Rees, Interview by Wright, 26 August 1983, adding that "the school turned inward," because "it was no longer the focus of national and international interest" it had been from 1957 to 1961.

It was a rough field in the fifties because people were coming up with new ideas and they were very salesmanship oriented. There were lots of polemics around, and a lot of claims that weren't valid . . . .[The information business] was a mess.[217]

Kent and Perry were extremely competent people. But the main thrust of their labors at Reserve "was to propagate a system which they felt to be a major solution to the literature problem."[218] In that regard, says Shera, "the center was a disappointment, and it was not until Perry and Kent left that I got it to do some of the things I wanted done . . . . They didn't give a hoot about the rest of the library school."[219] The documentation center, following their departure, "has become incorporated into the academic program of the school" as Shera originally intended.[220]

For all of the center's impressive successes in the fifties and early sixties, "traditional librarianship has always been the solid foundation of the school's program,"[221] and Shera refused to abandon it. He was unable to control Perry and Kent in the end; but his desire to enrich library education by involving it in communications research through new courses and conferences was indeed realized.

---

[217] Shera, Interview by Helmuth (1970).
[218] Rees, "Jesse H. Shera," 107.
[219] Shera, Interview by Helmuth (1970).
[220] Rees, "Jesse H. Shera," 107.
[221] Cramer, 100.

CHAPTER 4
THE SCHISM BETWEEN INFORMATION SCIENCE AND LIBRARIANSHIP

The Proper Position of Science

Shera's accomplishments clearly rose to the surface of troubled waters. Documentation was extremely important to him; but he deplored the tendency of the documentation center to become the tail that not only wanted to wag the dog but threatened to devour it. The stormy liaison of the center with the school, moreover, was becoming a microcosm for the similar relations of information science with librarianship generally.

Shera was profoundly disturbed by the turbulence of those relationships, and in his last published statement he faults information science for a large part of it. This statement, while severely critical, is very far from being a complete repudiation of information science, although it "represents a point of view that is not universally held by librarians . . . [and] information scientists."[222] He argues, for example, that information science is only the latest of many "attempts to . . . [improve] library technology and give it . . . respectability by endowing it with a unique name."[223] Those attempts can be traced to the beginnings of documentation, which arose in Europe when innovative librarians began using the Universal Decimal Classification (UDC) as a new technology for improving the ability of librarianship to access an increasingly complex range of international library materials. "These [library] pioneers relied on librarianship for their basic principles" without creating a new field of endeavor. "They [only] elaborated what had already been done. That they called themselves documentalists . . . did not change their objectives" or the nature of librarianship one whit.[224] When this movement came to America, the librarians who were interested in microphotography began calling themselves documentalists, for they, too, "had adopted a new technology;" but once again, there was no change in the nature or in the goals of

---

[222] Jesse H. Shera, "Librarianship and Information Science," in *The Study of Information*, Fritz Machlup and Una Mansfield, eds., (New York: Wiley, 1983), 379.
[223] Ibid., 381.
[224] Ibid., 380.

librarianship.[225] There was a pronounced change, however, in their condescending attitude toward the other librarians.

> Because these American documentalists, most of whom were librarians, based their technology on the science of photography, they tended to regard themselves as scientists . . . [avoided] the term *librarian*, and formed the American Documentation Institute (ADI). Thus began the fragmentation that has plagued librarianship ever since.[226]

American librarianship, that is to say, was not infected by science through the ADI: it was infected with *scientism*, the progressive librarian's unscientific worship of science as the sacred religion of the new librarianship. This malignancy, once introduced, has grown like a prairie fire consuming everything in its path. The revised version of the ADI, which adopted yet another new technology for retrieving information from knowledge records, was also "largely composed of librarians, with the addition of . . . [representatives from a few] commercial organizations, such as Eastman Kodak, Remington Rand, and General Electric."[227]

The breach between librarians and documentalists was beginning to widen: "librarianship was becoming a tarnished word," for the second wave of documentalists also "wanted to dissociate themselves from it."[228] The third wave of documentalists in the late sixties, moreover, so resented the contamination of documentation by librarianship that "the ADI changed its name to the American Society for Information Science;"[229] and since then, it has been the information scientists who have polarized with the librarians. "Today," says Shera, "even the Special Libraries Association . . . is contemplating a change of name" in order to describe its membership as something like "an association of information managers. The flight from *library* goes on, leaving the old and respected name to typify, in the main, public library service."[230]

Librarians have thus become the lepers of information management, and the justification for withdrawing from them is always

---

[225] Ibid.
[226] Ibid. Italics his.
[227] Ibid., 380-81, adding that these commercial organizations "had research resources far beyond those of librarians."
[228] Ibid., 381.
[229] Ibid.
[230] Ibid. Italics his.

the adoption of a new technology for improving access to knowledge. No discipline has arisen to replace librarianship, meanwhile, nor have there been any basic changes in its functions, purposes, goals, or essential nature. The whole case for information science and its antecedents turns on the fulcrum of scientific technology; and "except for some tinkering with its processes," Shera reminds us, "scientific technology has made but little contribution to the development of the library."[231]

The Nature of Professionalism

Because Shera understood this clearly, he reversed his thinking about information science in centrally significant ways. He knew instinctively what Flexner had stated in 1915, namely, that no profession can build itself upon its instruments. Technology is important in medicine and engineering, for example. "But in neither of these instances does the [professional] activity derive its essential character from its instruments; the instrument is an incident or an accident" of the critical thinking which controls its use. "No merely instrumental or mechanical activity can fairly lay claim to professional rank."[232]

Shera concluded, therefore, that "information science," insofar as it rests on purely technological foundations, "cannot qualify as a theoretical base for librarianship, and calling it bibliometrics or informatics [or anything else] does not alter the situation."[233]

> Twenty years ago, I thought of what is now called information science as providing the intellectual and theoretical foundations of librarianship, but I am now convinced that I was wrong. . . . I seriously question whether there is a true interdisciplinary relation between librarianship and information science; . . . [that relationship] is only a series of borrowings of the technology of one for the use of the other. Because librarianship is much more than . . . mechanized access to data

---

[231] Ibid., 385.
[232] Abraham Flexner, "Is Social Work a Profession?" *School and Society* 1 (1915): 902-3, adding that even "the execution or application of a well-thought out technique . . . is, after all, routine; someone back of the routineer has done the thinking . . . , and he alone deserves to be considered professional.
[233] Shera, "Librarianship and Information Science," 286. For more information on the dozens of other names for information science, see Machlup and Mansfield, 6-7.

banks or networks ..., we must look to other disciplines for its interdisciplinary relations and the core of its theory.[234]

In spelling out this significant reversal, which actually began shortly after the computer became operational at Reserve, Shera draws freely on two of my articles, "Professionalism and the Socratic Paradox"[235] and "The Instrumentality of Data."[236] I have therefore amplified some of his quotations from these articles and documented their sources in order to clarify this unorthodox way of thinking. Shera realized full well that the organizations, operations, functions, purposes, goals, and services of librarianship are most reducible to machinery. Professionalism, furthermore, is not derived from the expert use of tools. There is more to professional technique than technology, for technique presupposes "skill or efficiency at a particular job, and ... efficiency depends on ... knowledge of the job in hand."[237]

Such are the implications of *arête*, the Greek word wrongly translated as "virtue" in the Socratic paradox that "virtue is knowledge." What Socrates meant by that statement is: "You can't be efficient unless you take the trouble to learn the job."[238] According to the Socratic paradox, therefore, professional technique rests on basic knowledge, because technique always presupposes a function determined by structure: you can't figure out the best way of doing something unless there is something specific to be done; and what anything can do depends on what it is.[239]

The professional worker, regardless of his field, thinks in terms of his *function*, not in terms of his tools. He must know three things about the actual work he does for the public: (1) *its formal structure*, or what the work *is*, (2) *its functional purpose*, or what the work is *for*, and (3) *its occupational technique*, or the best way of performing the work. Otherwise, according to Socrates, the worker is incompetent. The technique of shoemaking, to use one of his favorite examples, depends on the shoemaker's possession of this knowledge: he cannot do his job

---

[234] Shera, "Librarianship and Information Science," 386.
[235] H. Curtis Wright, "Professionalism and the Socratic Paradox," *Scholar and Educator* 4 (Spring, 1980): 5-14.
[236] H. Curtis Wright, "The Instrumentality of Data," *National Librarian* 6 (May, 1981): 3-9.
[237] W. K. C. Gutherie, *The Greek Philosophers from Thales to Aristotle* (New York: Harper and Row, 1960): 9.
[238] Ibid., 10.
[239] Cf. ibid., 108-9: "The proper performance of function depends on structure.... Everything has its proper *ergon* [function].... Therefore everything has its proper *arête* [technique] ... the condition in which it can best perform its *ergon*."

professionally unless he can explain in simple language what shoemaking is and why the public he serves should find it useful.

> If you want to be a good shoemaker, he said, the first thing necessary is to know what a shoe is and what . . . [a shoe] is . . . for. It is no use trying to decide on [your shoemaking technique by selecting] the best . . . tools and materials to use and the best methods of using them unless you have first formed . . . a clear and detailed idea of what it is you are setting out to produce and what function it will have to perform.[240]

What, then, is the "shoe" of the particular "shoemaker" known as a librarian? Shera argues that it is an idea service based on the acquisition, organization, and interpretation of knowledge records.[241] Information science can help with problems in the operational or mechanistic sphere of knowledge organization by providing "ways in which the accumulated materials [of knowledge] can be arranged and processed for maximum convenience and efficiency of use;" but, says Shera, "it is here, and *only* here, that information science makes its contribution to librarianship;"[242] it cannot interpret the meanings of knowledge or determine the uses that can or should be made of it.

"Information science," he says, "deals with only a part of what the librarian does;" and therefore, "if librarians persist in sublimating librarianship to the lure of the machine and [to] the all-importance of data retrieval their 'shoes' will be . . . uncomfortable to the user, and they will leak at . . . vital points."[243]

A Holistic View of Librarianship

Shera has always argued for "the essential unity of librarianship with its offspring," which includes "a holistic view of librarianship," itself as well as its historical unity with "special librarianship, documentation, information retrieval and information science."[244] But this is no undifferentiated unity: it constitutes a psychophysical unity of immaterial realities (ideas) and physical instruments (data) in which two

---

[240] Ibid., 72.
[241] Shera, "Librarianship and Information Science," 384-45.
[242] Ibid., 385. Italics his.
[243] Ibid., 379, 385.
[244] Alan M. Rees, "Jesse H. Shera: A Reminiscence," *Information* 3 (March-April 1971): 107.

great halves interact to create the integrated unity of one great whole. "Information science . . . is not antithetical to librarianship," he says.[245]

They are children of the same parents, so why don't they love one another? The reasons are many and complex, but one of them is surely the twentieth-century librarian's lop-sided devotion to the assumptions and methods of science. "We need not be surprised," Shera observes, that the prewar "librarians rushed to embrace science and began to talk glibly of library science, turning their backs on the library's humanistic origins;" and the postwar "librarians even went so far as to evolve a new discipline called information science."[246]

This trip from humanism to science to library science to information science is problematic, because librarianship "is not, and never has been, a scientific enterprise."[247] It has a great deal of use for science, of course, which is precisely Shera's point: science in librarianship is an *instrument* for the use of librarians in pursuing their goals and performing their functions. "A catalog entry on the face of a cathode ray tube is essentially the same entry devised by Charles A. Cutter, and the fact that it has been transmitted across the continent in a fraction of a second may be a convenience to the user, but it does not alter the character of librarianship or transform it into a science."[248]

> Information science can provide the librarian with . . . important and useful tools to expedite library services, but the ability to communicate a message with incredible speed over long distances through the use of glass fiber bundles or laser beams or to store vast quantities of recorded knowledge in computerlike mechanisms does not in any way alter the purpose of the library. That the internal combustion engine can move . . . materials and people . . . with greater efficiency than the horse does not alter the need for transportation. The social purpose of the library remains unchanged--to bring the human mind and the graphic record together in a fruitful relation. . . . Administration, management, architecture, and many other disciplines can contribute to the effectiveness of the library, but they are not librarianship. . . . The librarian needs to attain . . .

---

[245] Jesse H. Shera, "Of Librarianship, Documentation, and Information Science," *UNESCO Bulletin for Libraries* 22 (1968): 65.
[246] Shera, "Librarianship and Information Science," 383.
[247] Ibid., 385. Cf. his negative review of Lloyd Houser and Alvin M. Schrader, *The Search for a Scientific Profession: Library Education in the U.S. and Canada* (Metuchen, N.J.: Scarecrow Press, 1977), *Library Quarterly* 49 (1979): 310-16. The review is negative because Shera regards the search itself as misconceived.
[248] Shera, "Librarianship and Information Science," 385.

specific skills in the *use* of the tools that all of these disciplines, including information science, have given us. But the hard core of librarianship remains basically as it has always been . . . , mastery of the substantive content of graphic records.[249]

The question facing librarians today, to summarize Shera's thought thus far, is not: "Is science relevant to librarianship?" The question is: "What *kind* of relevance does science have for librarianship?" And the answer is that science must play an instrumental role in subserving the functions and purposes of the library profession. Science can help librarians with their communicative tooling, in other words; but that's *all* it can do for them, because science belongs in the toolbox--not in the driver's seat--of librarianship.

Shera worried about the precarious relationship, lest his experience with the take-over mentality of tough-minded documentalists at Reserve become generalized throughout the profession. The paradox of this relationship is that the librarians, who should be in the driver's seat, want to be in the toolbox, whereas the information scientists, who ought to be in the toolbox, want to be in the driver's seat. Information science has never accepted its proper instrumental status in librarianship. It therefore rejects even the slightest hint of an ancillary role for science and asserts the scientific doctrine that knowledge is power as a means of subordinating librarianship to its own functions and purposes. The result is a power struggle, much like the microcosm at Reserve, in which there are no Jesse Sheras around to prevent the take-over.

Information science has therefore emerged victorious, and librarianship has been subjected to the indiscriminate pursuit of scientific objectives for their own sake. Librarianship is currently selling out to information science; and the librarians are fast forgetting, if they have not already forgotten, that "science is [merely] a subculture among subcultures,"[250] that it is only one way of thinking about the world, and that there are indeed other ways of thinking and other things to think about.

---

[249] Ibid., 387. Italics his.
[250] Kenneth E. Boulding, *The Image* (Ann Arbor, Michigan: University of Michigan Press, 1959): 16. Cf. also the rather devastating criticism of the extreme subjectivity of science in his *Economics as a Science* (New York: McGraw-Hill, 1970).

Drawbacks of Information Science

Because Shera saw this happening before he died, his last statement includes a number of interesting propositions about information science. Some of them, in addition to those already mentioned, are as follows:

1. <u>Information science has yet to prove itself as a discipline</u>. "It is still largely an agglomeration of technologies drawn from other areas of study, particularly . . . from mathematics and electrical engineering."[251]

2. <u>Computers must be adapted to the needs of librarians</u>, not the other way around. "We . . . say that the computer is here to stay and we must . . . adapt to its powers and capabilities . . . . The situation is quite the reverse: the computer is here to stay; therefore it must . . . adapt to the librarians' problems and needs."[252]

3. <u>Information science has a deepening identity crisis</u>.

   a. "Information science itself does not know what it is or where it is going. It cannot tell whether it belongs in a school of library science, [in] engineering, management, [or] operations research, or [in] some loosely defined area of its own."[253]
   b. "There is already distinct evidence that the American Society for Information Science is fragmenting itself into a variety of activities, some of which are mutually contradictory."[254]
   c. "The new technology is increasingly of interest to women."[255]

4. <u>Information science should be a research adjunct of librarianship</u>.

   a. *"Information science is an area of inquiry, of research.* It is not, as is librarianship, a service or a practice."[256]
   b. "We could say . . . that librarianship is a service and information science is an area of inquiry that seeks to measure and improve the efficiency of the librarian."[257]

---

[251] Shera, "Librarianship and Information Science," 379.
[252] Ibid., 384. Italics his.
[253] Ibid., 386.
[254] Ibid.
[255] Ibid., 382. This is based on employment figures for the members of the American Society of Information Scientists and the American Documentation Institute.
[256] Ibid., 387.

c. "We somewhat glibly assert that librarianship is a field of practice whereas information science is an area of research; and [so] it was in the early days. But today, if the membership of ASIS is indicative, information science is approaching an area of service not unlike that of librarianship. Both . . . are concerned with the transfer (I prefer the term *communication*) of . . . information (and again, I prefer *knowledge*). Information science, however, gets bigger headlines because of . . . engineering and mathematics in its technology."[258]

The Definition of Information

It was librarians, Shera reminds us, who "eagerly seized *information science* as potential supports to their . . . professionalism."[259] But information science, he says, has "misinterpreted Shannon and Weaver's specialized use of the noun *information* and assumed that it related to the communication of knowledge rather than the transmission of signals."[260] This has created a genuine problem for librarianship, because Shannon was interested *solely* in creating a theory of physical signals for describing "the message-carrying capacity of a symbol, a telephone wire, or any other medium or channel of communication."[261]

Thus, the theory he created was neither a theory of information nor a theory of communication: it was a technological theory of the physical means by which information is communicated. "Shannon specifically disavowed any pertinence of his mathematical . . . theory . . . for human communication," and Wiener did the same thing with information theory.[262]

It is therefore no accident that information theory "was never quite applicable to human communication systems," because Shannon, who intentionally excluded the human communicator from his mathematical model of communication, "made some assumptions

---

[257] Ibid., adding that this statement, although true, is inadequate because "information science deals with only a part of what the librarian does."
[258] Ibid., 382. Italics his.
[259] Ibid., 384, adding that "science does not a profession make, and an overlay of scientific operations is not a *sine qua non* for professionalism." Italics his.
[260] Ibid., 383, referring to Claude Shannon and Warren Weaver, the co-authors of *The Mathematical Theory of Communication* (Urbana: University of Illinois Press, 1949).
[261] Shera, "Of Librarianship, Documentation and Information Science," 62.
[262] Lee Thayer, *Communication and Communication Systems* (Homewood, Illinois: Richard D. Irwin, 1968): 189.

[about the mechanical senders and receivers of information] that are not exactly tenable for human systems."[263] Those assumptions stem from the mathematical concept of information invented by telephone engineers, which has never had anything to do with information in the ordinary sense of the term. "It is not . . . information as we usually understand it," says Miller, who always uses the word "in the technical sense first suggested by Hartley in 1928 and later developed by Shannon." Information in the technical sense always refers to "the degrees of freedom that exist [for a mechanical system] in any given situation to choose among signals, symbols, messages, or patters to be transmitted."[264] The physical symbol, in other words, has no symbolic referent in Hartley's technical concept of information, which "relates only to the signs themselves and does not relate to what they 'mean'." Hartley thus defined information, like Shannon and others who followed him, as the mechanical transmitter's "successive selection of signs, rejecting all meaning as a mere subjective factor" and insisting that "the signs must not be confused with the things they 'stand for.'"[265]

This way of thinking about information as physical data has nothing whatever in common with thinking about ideas. It was originally conceived in completely physical terms by Hartley, who, "in estimating the capacity of the physical system to transmit [what he called] information," argued that "we should ignore the question of interpretation," because "by this means the psychological factors . . . are eliminated and it becomes possible to set up a definite quantitative measure of information based on physical consideration alone."[266]

That is exactly what happened with the rise of information theory: information as the invisible structure of thought suddenly became information as the observable functions of matter-energy; and a word was no longer an abstraction with meaning, but "an acoustic or electrical disturbance which may be expressed as . . . an oscillographic

---

[263] D. J. Darnell, "Information Theory: an Approach to Human Communication," in *Interdisciplinary Approaches to Human Communication*, R. W. Budd and B. D. Ruben, eds. (Rochelle Park, NJ: Hayden Book Co., 1979): 158. Shannon's assumptions are discussed in Darnell, 160-61. On Shannon's exclusion of the human communicator, see R. L. Ackoff and F. E. Emery, *On Purposeful Systems* (Chicago: Aldine-Atherton, 1972): 11.
[264] J. G. Miller, *Living Systems* (New York: McGraw-Hill, 1978): 11. This *magnum opus* answers every question anyone can reasonably ask about systems theory.
[265] Colin Cherry, *On Human Communication: A Review, a Survey, and a Criticism* (3rd e.; Cambridge, Massachusetts: Massachusetts Institute of Technology Press, 1978), 50-51.
[266] R. V. L. Hartley, "Transmission of Information," *Bell System Technical Journal* 7 (1928): 538. This kind of physical thinking pervades the entire article.

record of a speech sound."[267] This is the technical concept of information originated by Hartley, developed by Shannon and Wiener, and refined by McGill and Ashby.[268]

"It is a pity," laments Colin Cherry, "that the mathematical concepts stemming from Hartley have been called 'information' at all."[269] That is precisely what reduces the study of ideas to action theory: thought becomes process so scientists can live with it. By and large, today's information professionals, whether librarians or information scientists, are philosophical materialists who define information as "a property of data . . . produced by a process that produced the data." Their physical thinking is transparent and complete, for the information process "may be simply *data transmission* . . . ; it may be *data selection*; it may be *data organization*; it may be *data analysis*."[270] But data it must be, one way or another, or it isn't information—which *therefore* has nothing to do with ideas.

The whole thing, says Shera, results from "an unfortunate use of terminology."[271] Information theorists currently use the term *information* "in a sense that has so little to do with any traditional or metaphoric meanings of the word that one can only wonder why the scientific community has allowed it to continue:" their reckless use of "information as an alias for signal transmission . . . has been infelicitous, misleading, and disserviceable, and . . . frequent attempts to correct this [deplorable] state of terminological affairs have been unsuccessful."[272]

Once Shannon's theory was firmly established, the almost mystical appeal of "information" became so attractive as to be well-nigh irresistible. "Everybody tried to get into the act" by applying his magic theory "to a wide range of disciplines" in "an intellectual get-rich-quick scheme" that could only end in the bankruptcy of confusion which

---

[267] Ibid., 582, adding that "such functions are also typical of other modes of communication."
[268] G. Broekstra, "On the Foundations of GIT," *Cybernetics and Systems: an International Journal* 11 (June-August, 1980): 11-12.
[269] Cherry, 51.
[270] Robert M. Hayes, "Information Science Education," in *ALA World Encyclopedia of Library and Information Science*, ed. R. Wedgeworth (Chicago: American Library Association, 1980), 249. For another of his process-oriented definitions of information as data, see R. M. Hayes and J. Becker, *Handbook of Data Processing for Libraries* (New York: Becker and Hayes, 1970), 745-47, which I have already opposed in my *The Oral Antecedents of Greek Librarianship* (Provo, Utah: Brigham Young University Press, 1978), xvi-xvii.
[271] Shera, "Of Librarianship, Documentation, and Information Science," 62.
[272] Fritz Machlup, "Semantic Quirks in Studies of Information," in *The Study of Information*, 658.

characterizes our thinking about information today.[273] "This extension of information theory . . . to other quite different fields [than engineering] has been a methodological disaster."[274]

The reductionist tendency of hard-core science, meanwhile, acknowledges no essential difference between data and ideas because it despises dichotomies and dualisms derived from the mind-body problem of philosophy. The resulting monistic "confusion between data and ideas," which regards data *as* ideas, "leads to the confusion between data systems and idea systems" that befuddles the information community today.[275] This confusion of ideas with data," says Shera, "Can be dispelled only by distinguishing between data systems and idea systems"[276]--a distinction the monistic materialists are unwilling to make.

"Our so-called information systems," he says, "are actually nothing but data systems,"[277] because they only "map the flow of *data* to or from humans or machines"[278] and cannot effect the transfer of ideas from one mind to another. Shera is here taking cues from Lee Thayer, who, though not an information scientist *per se*, is an important communications theorist of the sort found in departments of communication. According to Thayer, if any of the objects or processes in the physical universe fall "within the limited range of our sensory equipment (with or without amplification or translation by some technological device)," those objects or processes "are . . . potential data for us."[279] So long as any of those objects or processes "are within range," and "in the physical form . . . [which enables them] to be registered by our sensory equipment . . . , they will impinge upon that [sensory] equipment as data available to us about some aspect of our internal or external environments."[280] These data, furthermore, must be carefully distinguished from information.

> Information, not data, is the raw material for thinking. . . . If someone says something to you . . . , that person's utterance is . . . data . . . Your sensory equipment translates the physical

---

[273] Jesse H. Shera and Donald B. Cleveland, "History and Foundations of Information Science," *Annual Review of Information Science and Technology* 12 (1977): 261.
[274] Fritz Machlup and Una Mansfield, "Cultural Diversity in Studies of Information," in *The Study of Information*, 56.
[275] Shera, "Librarianship and Information Science," 384.
[276] Ibid., 386.
[277] Ibid., 386.
[278] Thayer, 116. Italics his.
[279] Ibid., 38.
[280] Ibid.

data of his speech [sounds] . . . into . . . neurological data. This neurological data is then . . . converted into . . . information. What your friend is actually producing--physical sound waves-- is now meaningful to you in the form of consumable . . . messages . . .

In . . . systems engineering and information . . . sciences, it is very useful for those concerned with human communication . . . to distinguish between that which is potentially available . . . [as] data . . . and that which is immediately consumable . . . [as] information. . . . Underlying all communication is the process of . . . converting raw sensory data into functionally-consumable . . . information. . . . .*It is indispensable to our understanding of human communication . . . to recognize this crucial difference between 'data' and 'information.'*[281]

A Choice for Librarians

Thayer is speaking here about the *human* communication of thought, not about the electronic or mechanical manipulation of data. That poses a fundamental problem for librarians: they will eventually have to decide, it seems, if they are interested primarily in the communication of knowledge-as-ideas (for which the controlled manipulation of data is instrumentation), or if they are solely concerned with the technology of communication.

There is no question about the choice Shera would have us make. The information scientists, he says, are "aligning themselves with the natural sciences, which deal with physical *phenomena*," [282] whereas "librarians . . . [deal] only incidentally with . . . [*phenomena*] but primarily with ideas, concepts, and thoughts. . . . The idea, not the process, is our primary concern."[283] Scientific theory "can be successfully applied to all technical problems concerning information;" but scientists "are in no position to investigate the process of thought," and they cannot entertain any theory "involving the human value of . . . information. This elimination of the human element," we are told, "is the price we have to . . . pay for . . . scientific knowledge."[284] That price, Shera finds, is much too high. The human element cannot be eliminated from librarianship, which "is much closer to the humanities than to the 'hard'

---

[281] Ibid., 29-30. Italics his.
[282] Jesse H. Shera, "Librarianship, Philosophy of," in *ALA World Encyclopedia*, 316.
[283] Shera, "Librarianship and Information Science," 384, 387.
[284] Leon Brillouin, *Science and Information Theory* (2nd e.; New York: Academic Press, 1963), x.

sciences,"[285] because librarians are, and must continue to be, "the guides to . . . mastery of the substantive content of graphic records."[286]

Information theory, furthermore, "cannot distinguish between information of great importance and . . . news of no great value."[287] The enthusiasm of his followers notwithstanding, Shannon's mechanistic assumptions about communications technology have severely limited the potential of information theory. Its purpose is to create a physical system which functions as the means of providing access to ideas; but the design, production, implementation, and control of the system get all of its attention. The schools of librarianship and information science are therefore turning out "control artists"--the data mechanics who tinker with information systems but stumble over the access problem because they can't control ideas. Thayer has explained the reason for all that by distinguishing between (1) communication and (2) communication systems.

> Information systems . . . are actually data transportation and data-processing systems. Their informational value is determined by . . . their data outputs [only as those outputs] are converted into information consumable by [people] . . .
>
> Even the most elaborate data systems do not guarantee that . . . intended communication will occur. . . . There is no data-handling procedure or electronic equipment which can obviate the fact that communication occurs only in people, not in the transportation or in the mechanical or electronic processing of data. . . . Communication does not occur in the . . . data. Communication. . . . occurs [only] *within* a consumer of the system's outputs, not in the system which transports data to him. Nor . . . is there any significance or meaning or utility in the data. . . . Communication . . . is a property of the consumer and the data flow combined--not of the data flow itself.[288]

The General Information Problem

In the last years of his life, Shera was deeply interested in issues like these. "The general information problem has three aspects," he told this writer in the early eighties, "and we have addressed only two of them." We have publicized the *sheer volume of information* as the now

---

[285] Shera, "Librarianship, Philosophy of," 316.
[286] Shera, "Librarianship and Information Science," 387.
[287] Brillouin, xi.
[288] Thayer, 115. Italics mine.

familiar knowledge explosion; and we have seemingly talked forever about the *fantastic growth in communications technology*, the means by which information is produced and processed in the physical world and transmitted throughout the natural universe; but we have neglected *the increasing involvement of the twentieth century with symbolism*, which is the basic cause of the knowledge explosion--the reason for both the imposing volume of information and the unprecedented growth of communications technology.

The information professionals have tried to deal scientifically with information by reducing symbolism to physical symbols-as-data in the form of printed characters (visible squiggles on paper), speech sounds (audible wrinkles in the atmosphere), or electro-chemical impulses (the circuitry of our nervous systems and computers). But there is more to symbolism than symbols, as information clearly transcends the data by means of which it is expressed. For every symbol in the physical environment of the natural universe, in other words, there is a symbolic referent in the intellectual environment of the cultural universe. The symbol and the symbolic referent thus belong to completely different orders of reality--which means that the symbolic process of information cannot be understood in the absence of a dualistic theory that explains exactly how symbols and symbolic referents are wired up to each other and to human beings.[289]

This brings us to the last proposition offered by Shera to the library profession. "I submit," he says, "that librarians must look to 'symbolic interactionism' for the proper foundation of a theory of librarianship."[290] Systems theory is the scientific way of accounting for the technical aspects of communication *systems*; it does not account for human communication. But symbolic interactionism, which "refers to the [psychophysical] process by which people relate to their own minds and the minds of others,"[291] is a very real alternative to systems theory, an alternative which provides the humanistic account of communication.

---

[289] This is the "jist," as near as I can remember it, of my telephone conversations with Shera in the early eighties. His ideas and mine are all mixed up together here, and I am not sure exactly which of us is responsible for what. Still, this gives the general drift of our conversations--which were pretty serious and very deep, I might add.
[290] Shera, "Librarianship and Information Science," 386.
[291] Ibid.

Symbolic Interactionism

Symbolic interactionism was created by George Herbert Mead, who rejected the study of social phenomena by mechanistic methods brought into sociology from physics but apparently despaired of doing anything about it outside of the classroom. When Mead died virtually unpublished in the early thirties, however, several of his books were published posthumously by his former students. His influence, which has grown steadily in sociology and social psychology ever since, underlies the essentially humanistic thinking of communication theorists like Lee Thayer.

Mead has thus arisen from the dead to plague the scientific sociologists by calling them to account for aping the manners of physics and assuming the identity of natural and social phenomena in their researches. The social order, unlike the natural order, is an ontological dualism constituted by (1) *an empirical social order*, which consists of people as behavers who do things, and (2) *an ideative social order*, which consists of people as thinkers who know things. Humanists regard the empirical social order as the only means of access to the ideative social order, whereas scientists treat the ideative social order as nonexistent and regard the empirical social order as a subset of the natural order. Science, that is to say, studies human behavior without reference to mind; but humanism studies man's behavior as the means of access to his mind.

Systems theory, which derives from scientific thinking, therefore concentrates perforce on the behavioral aspects of communication without considering its ideative aspects. Symbolic interactionism, however, investigates the psychophysical interaction of the empirical order and the ideative order in human beings by studying the relationship between the physical symbol and its symbolic referent. It regards human interaction as essentially social and symbolic, for "nearly every movement, sound, odor, or touch of another human being acts as a symbol which we learn to interpret" by attaching subjective meanings to it.[292]

This clarifies the informational function of physical symbols-as-data in communication: the meanings we see in the data are in us, not in the data. We create symbolism by attaching meanings to data and using them as instruments of communication; and communication is impossible unless the data are made to function instrumentally (and

---

[292] James P. Spradley, "Foundations of Cultural Knowledge," in *Culture and Cognition*, James P. Spradley, ed. (San Francisco: Chandler, 1972), 16.

invisibly) as symbolic signs: they must suggest ideas to the mind without getting in the way. Symbolic interactionism, says Shera, "reminds librarians that their area of concern is based on social phenomena," not on natural phenomena.[293]

And we need reminding. We live in a day when scientific philosophies of humanism are fashionable; but everybody gets nervous when someone like George Herbert Mead or Karl Popper comes up with provocative and seminal ideas based on a humanistic philosophy of science. "We librarians," Shera says, "must constantly remind ourselves that our concern is with the sociological and psychological phenomena, not [with] physical objects and processes."[294]

> The library looks in two directions simultaneously. It looks toward the social sciences, because it is a creature of society.... Thus, the library qualifies as a social agency or instrumentality. But the library is also humanistic in that its characteristics, [its] modes of access to its resources, [its] uses, and [its] values are humanistic.[295]

It is impossible, as a matter of fact, to imagine anything more thoroughly humanistic than librarianship. But librarianship is currently being dehumanized by information science, with its strong empirical emphasis on physical symbols and its corresponding inability to manage the intellectual realities of symbolic referents. Librarians have traditionally confused communication with the behavior of physical symbols; but the postwar librarians have pushed that confusion to its ultimate limits: they can't tell the difference anymore between information science, which is based on the controlled manipulation of data, and librarianship, which is based on the intersubjective communication of ideas. They have sacrificed their essential humanism on the altar of high technology by capitulating to systems theory, the scientific way of accounting for the empirical *phainomena* of communication; and they know virtually nothing about symbolic interactionism, the humanistic way of accounting from the intellectual *noumena* of communication.

There are thus *two* theoretical perspectives on the realities of communication, for systems theory and symbolic interactionism are not merely rival theories of communication: they are theoretical *perspectives* which constitute radically different approaches to the whole problem of

---

[293] Shera, "Librarianship and Information Science," 387.
[294] Ibid., 386.
[295] Ibid., 385.

theorizing about communication. The scientific and humanistic perspectives thus constitute the necessary dipoles of communication theory which serve as the general orientations for all possible theories of communication; and it is not going too far to say that every theory of communication known to date is built on one of these two perspectives or is a combination of both. It is abundantly clear, therefore, that general systems theory, which deals with physical symbols, can never replace symbolic interactionism, which deals with the psychophysical *interaction* of physical symbols with their ideative referents. It is also clear that the librarian's enthusiastic endorsement of the former and continuing indifference to the latter are grossly and thoroughly indefensible.[296]

Pragmatism and Anti-intellectualism

Finally, Shera ends his lifelong involvement in librarianship with a parting swipe at the simplicity of library pragmatism and a warning about computers. That's where we shall end after commenting on the relationship between pragmatism and anti-intellectualism in American librarianship today. The following quotation is from Shera, and what follows the quotation is this writer's commentary on Shera.

> In the American character, there has [always] been a strong strain of . . . pragmatism, and this is . . . clearly evident . . . in librarianship. The major figures in . . . American librarianship were doers rather than thinkers; they were concerned with process rather than purpose. They devised and taught in their library schools routines and procedures, and with the advent of online networks and access to data banks, they are doing it more than ever today.[297]

This statement should be familiar to librarians, as Shera has made similar statements before. What may not be familiar to those unfamiliar with philosophy, however, is the fact that pragmatism and anti-intellectualism are more or less synonymous, as are their antonyms, rationalism and intellectualism. The overly pragmatic outlook of American librarianship in all things, which merely reflects the all-inclusive nature of the larger American pragmatism, is responsible for

---

[296] For additional information on this topic see: Vernon W. Larsen and H. Curtis Wright, "Symbolic Interaction Theory," *Scholar and Educator* XI: 1-2 (Spring 1987): 49-78.
[297] Shera, "Librarianship and Information Science," 383.

the vigorous anti-intellectualism of today's librarians.[298] According to William James, not until his own day had pragmatism "generalized itself, become conscious of a universal mission, pretended to a conquering destiny. I believe in that destiny," he says--and so do the librarians he inspired with that belief.[299]

Pragmatism is the beloved national philosophy of America, and attacking it can be as dangerous as criticizing baseball or apple pie. Hunt defends it as "plausible reasoning," for example, which permits us, when faced with a problem, "to make skilled guess at an answer" without coming "to that answer by formal deductive means;" he even calls it "our *natural* mode of reasoning," arguing that "we are pragmatists by nature" and that "our pragmatism . . . is not anti-intellectual" because it constitutes the kind of "effective intellectuality" that appeals to practical people everywhere.[300]

For all that, however, pragmatism and anti-intellectualism are so similar as to be almost identical. We find "the signs of revolt against intellectualism" in scores of writers;[301] but "in James pragmatism [actually] becomes a revolt against 'intellectualism' because he tacitly identified this with rationalism."[302] And James despised rationalism: it "is far too intellectualistic" for pragmatism, which therefore "turns her back upon the intellectualist point of view altogether."[303]

Thus pragmatism suggests anti-intellectualism. Anti-intellectualism, meanwhile, also smacks of pragmatism, for it "suggests the revulsion from ideology and the *a priori*, from the abstract thought of the century and a half preceding [the 1890s] . . . . It recalls the influence and prestige of William James," which extends to writers as different as Durkheim and Sorel.[304] Pragmatism is notorious for exalting action over thought; and anti-intellectualism "is virtually equivalent to

---

[298] Cf. D. Isaacson, "Anti-intellectualism in American Libraries," *Library Journal* 107 (Feb 1, 1982): 227-32; and L. Dee Garrison, "The Tender Technicians," *Journal of Academic Librarianship* 3 (1977): 10-19.

[299] William James, *Pragmatism: a New Name for Some Old Ways of Thinking* (Cambridge, Massachusetts: Harvard University Press, 1978), 30, who argued that the older pragmatists "were preluders only," that is that he (James) was the great high priest of the new and improved religion of purified pragmatism.

[300] Morton Hunt, *The Universe Within* (New York: Simon and Schuster, 1982): 137-38. Italics mine.

[301] Boris Sokoloff, *The 'Mad' Philosopher: Auguste Comte* (New York: Vantage Press, 1961): 10.

[302] J. H. Randall and J. Buchler, *Philosophy: an Introduction* (New York: Vantage Press, 1961): 10.

[303] James, 39, 62.

[304] H. Stuart Hughes, *Consciousness and Society* (New York: Knoff, 1958), 36.

Jamesian pragmatism"[305]--although many pragmatists resented (and continue to resent) that term for describing their tough-minded philosophy.[306] All of the above, furthermore, was acknowledged by William James himself, who placed pragmatism squarely in the mainstream of philosophical materialism:

> It agrees with [materialistic] nominalism . . . in always appealing to particulars; with [materialistic] utilitarianism in emphasizing practical aspects; with [materialistic] positivism in its disdain for verbal solutions, useless questions, and metaphysical abstractions.
>
> All these [variants of materialism], you see, are *anti-intellectualist* tendencies. Against rationalism as a pretension and a method, pragmatism [as a pretension and a method] is fully armed and militant . . . . It has no dogmas, and no doctrines save its [materialistic] method.[307]

Despite its widespread acceptance among information professionals, therefore, pragmatism is an indefensible philosophical stance in the librarian for two reasons: (1) it constitutes an experientially biased philosophy of action derived from scientific materialism;[308] and (2) librarians are in the knowledge business, not in the action business. The gut-mistake of the American librarians is the forlorn attempt to reduce their knowledge problems to action theory in order to solve them scientifically. But action theory cannot resolve the knowledge problems of librarianship because theories of knowledge (epistemology) are not reducible to theories of action (ethics/societology/science) or vice versa; and the net result of their historic failure to resolve knowledge problems scientifically is the measure of their anti-intellectualism.

---

[305] Ibid., 36.
[306] Ibid., 176-77.
[307] James, 32. Italics his.
[308] Ibid., 126, 133. See also T. V. Smith, "The Scientific Way of Life with William James as Guide," chapter 3 of his *The Philosophical Way of Life in America* (2nd ed.; New York: F. S. Crofts, 1943), 51-80.

CHAPTER 5
CONCLUSION

The American librarians had always used a Model-T technology for getting where they needed to go when the engineers suddenly gave them the most powerful and sophisticated Cadillac technology imaginable. They were frustrated by the Cadillac at first (because they didn't know how to use it), and then fascinated with it (because it had so many advantages over the Model-T). But they tended, as they learned to use it, to become interested in the Cadillac as a means of going *anywhere* and forgetful as to where they should be going.

The new technology, Shera thinks, is to be used for the librarian's purposes, not for the purposes of its designers or manufacturers, and certainly not for its own purposes. A Cadillac is a sophisticated piece of equipment; but neither it nor the Model-T can tell librarians whether they should go to Chicago or not or when to turn off the freeway. Those prerogatives belong to the librarians, and they must not forfeit them to others.

Shera is worried, it seems, about the take-over mentality of the information scientists, lest they wrest control of the Cadillac, to say nothing of librarianship, from the librarians. "The great danger with which information science threatens librarianship," he warns, "is . . . loss of control of the profession to other and less competent hands. Of the dangers inherent in this threat," he adds, "we do not now seem to be fully aware."[309]

Librarianship is a trinity of acquisition, organization, and knowledge service, according to Shera; but information science contributes to librarianship *only* in matters of organization--by arranging and processing its accumulated materials "for maximum convenience and efficiency of use."[310] The information scientists must not interfere with the library's reason for being, however, which is the provision of knowledge service based on the interpretation of ideas. "It is here," says Shera, "that information science reveals its greatest threat of dehumanizing the library's function."[311]

---

[309] Shera, "Librarianship and Information Science," in *The Study of Information*, Fritz Machlup and Una Mansfield, eds. (New York: Wiley, 1983), 387.
[310] Ibid., 385.
[311] Ibid.

There is more to information science than the computer; everyone knows that. Still, information science minus the computer is pretty close to nothing. Shera has consistently warned librarians "against becoming 'punch--drunk' from . . . [technology] and forgetting that 'machines are only so much intricate and spectacular hardware if they are improperly designed for the task they are supposed to perform and if their capabilities and limitations . . . are imperfectly understood.'"[312] We are in serious trouble if the means of doing our job becomes the job we are doing. "The basic purpose of librarianship is not encompassed in the machine, and there is much more to librarianship than is envisaged in information science."[313]

> The new technology, the brightly shining new machines with their spinning reels of tape, [and] the finely spun theories of information science are but means to an end. They can do no more than increase . . . accessibility to recorded knowledge.[314]

There are bad things in store, Shera feels, "if we permit ourselves to be mesmerized by the gadget" or to "accept the flickering image of data on a fluorescent screen as knowledge."[315] Popper was right: the computer, even with its shimmering images, "is just a glorified pencil" after all.[316]

Einstein said once, "my pencil is smarter than I am."[317] Einstein with a pencil was a lot sharper than Einstein without a pencil, there's no doubt about that. But even our pencils can get out of hand--if we let them go to our heads. They are like the sorcerer's broom.

I remember vaguely, from somewhere in my childhood, the story of a boy about my age who was apprenticed to a sorcerer. One day, when he was alone in the shop, the boy managed to bewitch the sorcerer's broom into doing his work for him by fetching water to fill a cistern. He was elated by what he got the broom to do until he tried to stop it because the cistern was full and discovered that he couldn't unbewitch it. He chopped the broom in half with an axe in order to stop it, but the halves became two brooms and carried twice as much

---

[312] Jesse H. Shera and Donald B. Cleveland, "History and Foundations of Information Science," *Annual Review of Information Science and Technology* 12 (1977): 259.
[313] Shera, "Librarianship and Information Science," 387.
[314] Shera, "Documentation into Information Science," *Strategies for Change in Information Programs*, William E. Hug, ed. (New York: Bowker, 1974), 285.
[315] Shera, "Librarianship and Information Science," 387.
[316] Karl R. Popper and John c. Eccles, *The Self and its Brain* (New York: Springer-Verlag, 1981), 208.
[317] Ibid., where Popper's translation is "my pencil is cleverer than I."

water to the cistern as before. So, the boy had to swim for his life or perish in the flood he caused and could not stop. The moral of that story is precisely Shera's point: our glorified pencil "must be kept in its proper place as a tool and a slave, or we will become sorcerer's apprentices, with data everywhere and not a thought to think."[318]

---

[318] Shera, "Librarianship and Information Science," 384.

CHRONOLOGICAL BIBLIOGRAPHY
The Published Works of Jesse Hauk Shera
(Arranged by Date of Publication)

Nota Bene.--I have listed these publications chronologically in order to facilitate preparations for writing a biography of Jesse Shera. This duplicates the previous arrangement of a ten-foot stack of documents, which organizes my careful selection of Shera's personal papers from the archives at Case Western Reserve University. These two files, plus data from such ancillary sources as personal interviews, constitute my *materia sherica*--the foundation on which I shall try to reconstruct the portrait of an important life. My intentions are twofold: (1) to read through both of these files simultaneously, beginning with the earliest available documents, proceeding item-by-item in strict chronological order (or as close to that order as possible), and ending with the latest available documents; and (2) to note and comment on anything that interests me along the way. Thus, the chronological arrangement of Shera's published works has an ulterior motive: it was prepared with a specific biographical method in view; and those who eschew that method are free to write their own biographies of Jesse Shera in any way they choose.

My way of listing dates in chronological order may be illustrated by my own birth date which, prior to World War II, consistently appeared in documents as February 16, 1928 (or in its abbreviated forms as Feb. 16, 1928, 2/16/28, or 2-16-28). During the war, however, the armed forces of the United States changed this month-day-year sequence of dating to a day-month-year sequence, and my birthday began showing up as 16 February 1928, 16 Feb. 1928, 16/2/28, or 16-2-28. I have staged a bibliographic coup in this matter and overthrown the military establishment by reversing its procedure and adopting a year-month-day sequence for arranging Shera's publications chronologically. But I have not done this in a nasty spirit of retaliation against Uncle Sam for the permanent ambiguity he has forced upon those unfortunate enough to be born between the 1st and 12th days of any month by introducing month-day (or is it day-month?) confusion into our dating arrangements. Who knows when three of my sons were born, for example, if I list their natal days as 2-10-61, 2-4-66, and 8-9-70? Or as 10-2-62, 4-2-66, and 9-8-70? I dislike multiple systems, bibliographically speaking, and deplore the fact that both datal procedures are thriving in the land--I have even thought of writing an article entitled "World War II as a Bibliographical Problem." But that was not my reason for arranging Shera's publications by a year-month-day sequence. I did it because I had already ordered his personal papers in that manner, and I wanted to arrange his publications in the same way.

The year-month-day sequence arranges documents chronologically according to the principle of maximum specificity. Thus, books are usually entered under the year of publication only (since they rarely mention the month or day when they appear), whereas articles are normally found under the year, the month, and often the very day when they were published. But the first item in the bibliography, which would normally be filed under "29" (for 1929), is listed under "29 Sep" (meaning September, 1929, not September 29th) because the document itself contains the note "Published September 1929; second printing, January 1930; third printing, October 1930." And there are other inconsistencies, many of which are caused by multiple entries under the same date. I have tried to resolve most of these by grouping them as separates (books, occasional papers, etc.), partials (chapters, reports, proceedings, introductions, forewords, prefaces, bibliographies, and other parts of separates), articles (in journals, encyclopedias, etc.), reviews (including review articles), and miscellaneous (for things like editorials and abstracts), in that order. I have also solved the problem of entries like "58 Winter" by arbitrarily filing them before entries like "58 Jan" (not before "58 Dec," or worse still, before "57 Dec"). Where "Autumn" and "Fall" have both been entered under the same date, I have arranged them alphabetically. There are doubtless other inconsistencies in a lengthy bibliography like this, which was compiled over a period of several years; but they can usually be resolved with a little judicious snooping through the multiple entries for a given day or month, or even for a given year in some cases.

I cannot claim that this bibliography is exhaustive, although it has certainly been exhausting; and I have indeed taken definite pains to make it as complete as possible. I therefore appeal to anyone who knows of anything at all published by Jesse Shera that does not appear in this list (especially if they know of any of his peripheral publications that have not made it into the mainline indexes and bibliographies) to contact me at 5042 HBLL, Brigham Young University, Provo, Utah, 84602. I would also be grateful to learn of any personal papers written either by or to Jesse Shera that are not already in my other file.

H. Curtis Wright
Brigham Young University
January, 1988

1929

29 Sept. "Bibliography." In *Danger Spots in World Population*, by Warren S. Thompson, 334-43. New York: Alfred A. Knopf, 1929. Third printing carries this note: "Published September 1929; second printing, January 1930; third printing, October 1930."

1930

30. "Bibliography." In *Population Problems*, by Warren S. Thompson, 427-45. New York: McGraw-Hill, 1930, 427-45. Shera is mentioned in the Preface as compiler of this bibliography. See 2d ed. (1935).

1931

31. "The Age Factor in Employment: a Classified Bibliography." *Bulletin of Bibliography* 14 #5 (1931): 100-101.

31. "The Age Factor in Employment: a Classified Bibliography." *Bulletin of Bibliography* 14 #6 (1931): 128-29.

31 Jan. "Handmaidens of the Learned World." *Library Journal* 56 (1931): 21-22.

31 Nov. "The Place of Library Service in Research: a Suggestion." *Libraries* 36 (1931): 387-90.

1932

32. "The Age Factor in Employment: a Classified Bibliography. *Bulletin of Bibliography* 14 #7 (1932): 154-56.

32. "The Age Factor in Employment: a Classified Bibliography. *Bulletin of Bibliography* 14 #8 (1932): 175-77.

32. "The Age Factor in Employment: a Classified Bibliography. *Bulletin of Bibliography* 14 #9 (1932): 193-95.

32 Sep. "The Removal of Shellac and Ink from the Backs of Leather-bound Volumes." *Wilson Bulletin* 7 (September, 1932): 32.

1933

33 Feb 15. "The Librarian's 'Changing World.'" *Library Journal* 58 (1933): 149-52.

33	Oct.	"Recent Social Trends and Future Library Policy." *Library Quarterly* 3 (1933): 339-53.

1934

34	Mar.	"Second Prize." [For an article of 500 words or less on the question: Should the preponderance of women in the American library profession be considered an evil?] *Wilson Bulletin for Librarians* 8 (March, 1934): 404-5 (*in context* pp. 230-31, 403-9).
34	Nov.	"Viewpoint Shift in Reference Work." *Special Libraries* 25 (1934): 235-37.

1935

35.		"Bibliography." In *Population Problems,* by Warren S. Thompson, 457-80. 2d ed. New York: McGraw-Hill, 1935. Shera is still mentioned in the Preface of the 2d ed. As the complier of its bibliography, which is dropped from later editions of this work. See 1st edition (1930).
35	Jan.	"An Eddy in the Western Flow of American Culture; the History of Printing and Publishing in Oxford, Ohio, 1827-1841." *Ohio State Archaeological and Historical Quarterly* 44 (1935), 103-127.
35	Jun.	"The 'Unaffiliated' Member and the SLA." *Special Libraries* 26 (1935): 124-25.
35	Dec.	"Member No. 3!" *Wilson Bulletin for Librarians* 10 (December 1935): 267-68.

1936

36	Jan.	Review of *Curse in the Colophon*, by Edgar J. Goodspeed. In *Library Journal* 61 (1936): 24.
36	Apr.	"Call to Action." *Wilson Bulletin for Librarians* 10 (April, 1936): 532-33.
36	Apr.	Review of *Social Change and Education. Thirteenth Yearbook . . .* Department of Superintendence of the National Education Association. In *ALA Bulletin* 31 #3 (March, 1937): 141-46.
36	Jun.	"The College Library of the Future." *ALA Bulletin* 30 (1936): 494-501.
36	Jun.	"Richmond--and Beyond." *Wilson Bulletin* 10 (1936): 648-49.

1937

37.   "Selected Bibliography." In *Research Memorandum on Internal Migration in the Depression*, by Warren S. Thompson, 69-82. Studies in the Social Aspects of the Depression. New York: Social Science Research Council, 1937. Shera's bibliography has here been augmented by a bibliography on migration by Dr. Dorothy Thomas. Reprinted 1972.

37	Mar.	"College Librarianship and Educational Reform." *ALA Bulletin* 31 (1937): 141-46.
37	May-Jun.	"Training for 'Specials': a Prologue to Revision." *Special Libraries* 28 (1937): 139-44.
37	Jun.	"An Exchange of Correspondence." *Wilson Bulletin for Librarians* 11 (June, 1937): 715-16.
37	Jun 22.	"Council Votes to Probe Civil Rights Cases." *Wilson Daily Bulletin* 2 (June 22, 1937): 1.
37	Jun 23.	"Salary Survey Endorsed by Tenure Committee." *Wilson Daily Bulletin* 3 (June 23, 1937): 8.
37	Jul.	"Barred Gates: a Librarian's Plea for Freedom." *PNLA Quarterly* 1 (1937): 54-55.
37	Nov.	"Training for 'Specials' the Status of the Library Schools." *Special Libraries* 28 (1937): 317-21.

1938

38	Mar.	**"Cooperative Book Club." *ALA Bulletin* 32 (March, 1938): 215-16.**
38	Mar.	"Swan Song of a Junior." *ALA Bulletin* 32 (March, 1938): 181-84.
38	Jul-Aug.	"And What of the Future?" Special Libraries 29 # 6 (July-August, 1938): 198-99.
38	Dec.	"The Strength of the Pack." *SLA Newsletter, Cincinnati Chapter,* (December, 1938) 2-3.

1939

39	Jan.	**"Accent on Youth; the Significance of A.L.A. Reorganization for the Young Librarian." *Wilson Bulletin* 13 (1939): 312-13, 324.**
39	Apr.	"Tomorrow, and Tomorrow, and Tomorrow." Review of *The Library of Tomorrow,* by Emily V. Danton. In *ALA Bulletin* 33 (1939): 249, 278.
39	Jun.	"A Few Coals to Newcastle." *Wilson Bulletin for Librarians* 13

9 (June, 1939): 702, 717.

1940

40	Apr.	Review of *The New England Hind: the Seventeenth Century,* by Perry Miller. New York: Macmillan, 1939. In *Library Quarterly 10* (1940): 302-6.
40	Oct.	Review of *Business and the Public Library: Steps in Successful Cooperation,* ed. Marian C. Manley. New York: Special Libraries Association, 1940. In *Library Quarterly* 10 (1940): 603-5.
40	Oct.	Review of *The Feminine Fifties,* by Fred Lewis Pattee. In *Library Quarterly* 10 (1940): 618-21.

1941

| 41 | Apr. | *Review of Cotton Mather: a Bibliography of his Works* by Thomas James Holmes. In *Library Quarterly* 11 (1941): 232-34. |

1942

| 42 | Jan. | Review of *The Sentimental Novel in America,* 1789-1860, *by Herbert Ross Brown.* In *Library Quarterly* 12 (1942): 133-36. |
| 42 | Oct. | Review of The Seventh Annual Report of the Archivist of the United States for the Fiscal Year ending June 30, 1941, by the National Archives. In *Library Quarterly* 12 (1942): 851-53. |

1943

43.		"Libraries and Museums." In Development of Collective Enterprise; Dynamics of an Emergent Economy, ed. Seba Eldridge, chapter 12, 183-207. Lawrence, Kansas: University of Kansas Press, 1943.
43	Mar.	Review of *The Growth of the American Republic,* by Samuel Eliot Morison and Henry Steele Commager. 3rd ed. In *Mississippi Valley Historical Review* 29 (1942-43): 580-81.
43	Sep.	Review of *The Growth of American Nationality, 1492-1865,* by Fred W. Wellborn. In *Mississippi Valley Historical Review* 30 (1943) 249-50.

1944

44.		"The Center of Documentation -- a Regional Approach." In *Documentation on a Regional Basis; Symposium on Post-war Activities,* by the Philadelphia Bibliographic Center and Union Library Catalogue, vi-ix. Philadelphia: The Center, 1944.
44	Mar.	"Special Library Objectives and Their Relation to Administration." *Special Libraries* 35 (1944), 91 - 94.
44	Jul.	Review of *The Growth of American Thought,* by Merle Curti. In *Library Quarterly* 14 (1944): 250-52.

1945

45	Jan.	"The Literature of American Library History." *Library Quarterly* 15 (1945): 1-24.
45	Mar.	Review of *Land of the Free: a Short History of the American People,* by Homer C. Hockett and Arthur M. Schlesinger. In *Mississippi Valley Historical Review* 31 (1944-45): 588-89.
45	Jul.	Review of *The Idea of Progress in America, 1815-1860,* by Arthur A. Ekirch. In *Library Quarterly* 15 (1945): 252-54.
45	Sep.	"Surplus Books Available from Army and Navy Instructional Programs." *College and Research Libraries* 6 # 4 (September, 1945): 376.
45	Sep.	Review of *Catalogers' and Classifiers' Yearbook No. 11, 1945,* comp. by the Division of Cataloging and Classification of the American Library Association. In *College and Research Libraries* 6 (1944-45): 371-72.

1946

46	Jan.	"Influences on American Culture." Review of *Foreign Influences* in *American Life: Essays and Critical Bibliographies,* ed. David F. Bowers. In *College and Research Libraries* 7 (1946): 95-96.
46	Apr.	Review of *The House of McMillan (1843-1943),* by Charles Morgan. In *Library Quarterly* 16 (1946), 173-75.
46	Jun.	Review of *The Cambridge Press, 1638-1692: a Reexamination of the Evidence concerning The Bay Psalm Book and the Eliot Indian Bible as well as Other Contemporary Books and People,* by George Parker Winship. In *Mississippi Valley Historical Review* 33 (1946-47): 158-59.

1948

48. "Administration of the Library--Technical Operations." In *Survey of the Saginaw Library System,* by Margaret E. Egan. Chicago: the Author, 1948, 103-27.

48 Apr. Review of *Harvard Library Bulletin,* vol. I, no. 1 (Winter, 1947). In *Library Quarterly* 18 (1948): 130.

48 Jul. Review of *A History of Libraries in Great Britain and North America,* by Albert Predeek. In *Library Quarterly* 18 (1948): 226-28.

48 Oct. Review of *The Vatican Library: Rules for the Catalog of Printed Books,* ed. Wyllis E. Wright. In *Library Quarterly* 18 (1948): 299-302.

1949

49. *Foundations of the Public Library: the Origins of the Public Library Movement in New England, 1629-1855.* **Chicago: University of Chicago Press, 1949.**

49 Winter. With Margaret Egan. "Prolegomena to Bibliographic Control." *Journal of Cataloging and Classification* 5 (1949): 17 - 19.

49 Apr 22. "A Summary of the Historical Background of Classification Theory," In *Symposium* on *Special Classification Systems,* by the U.S. Research and Development Board, Special Committee on Technical Information, 1-6. Washington, D. C.: U. S. Research and Development Board, 1949.

49 Jul. Review of *Documentation,* by S. C. Bradford. In *College and Research Libraries* 10 (1949): 276-77.

49 Jul. Review of *Library and Reference Facilities in the Area of the District of Columbia,* 3d ed., issued by the Library of Congress, Reference Department, Loan Division. In *Library Quarterly* 19 (1949): 216-17.

49 Oct. Review of *Cataloguing: a Textbook for Use in Libraries,* by Henry A. Sharp. In *Library Quarterly* 19 (1949): 304-5.

49 Oct. Review of *Fundamentals of Practical Cataloguing,* by Margaret S. Taylor. In *Library Quarterly* 19 (1949): 304-5.

1950

50. With Margaret E. Egan. "The United States Report on National and International Bibliographic Problems." Chicago: Graduate Library School,

		University of Chicago, 1950. Mimeographed.
50	Jan.	With Margaret E. Egan. "Documentation in the United States." *American Documentation* 1 # 1 (January, 1950): 8-12.
50	Jan.	"Upon First Looking into John Cook Wyllie's 'The Need.'" *College and Research Libraries* 11 (January, 1950): 85.
50	Mar.	Review of *The Papers of Thomas Jefferson,* vol. I, eds. Julian P. Boyd *et al. Minnesota History* 31 (March, 1950): 179-80.
50	Apr.	Review of *ALA Cataloging Rules for Author and Title Entries,* prepared by the Division of Cataloging and Classification of the American Library Association, Clare Beetle, ed. *Library Quarterly* 20 # 2 (April, 1950): 147-50.
50	Apr.	Review of *Rules for Descriptive Cataloging in the Library of Congress,* issued by the Descriptive Cataloging Division, U. S. Library of Congress. In *Library Quarterly* 20 # 2 (April, 1950): 147-50.
50	Apr.	Review of *The Story of Illinois,* by Theodore Calvin Pease. In *Ohio State Archaeological and Historical Quarterly* 59 # 2 (April 1950): 217-19.
50	Apr.	Review of *This is Illinois; a Pictorial History,* by Jay Monaghan. In *Ohio State Archaeological and Historical Quarterly* 59 # 2 (April, 1950): 217-19.
50	Aug.	"The UNESCO Conference on the Improvement of Bibliographic Services; a Preliminary Report." *American Documentation* 1 # 3 (August, 1950): 144-46.
50	Aug.	With Margaret E. Egan. "The United States Report on National and International Bibliographic Problems." *American Documentation* 1 # 3 (August, 1950): 146-51.
50	Oct.	With Margaret E. Egan. Review of *Principles of Bibliographical Description,* by Fredson Bowers. *College and Research Libraries* 11 # 4 (October, 1950): 399-401.
50	Oct.	With Margaret E. Egan. Review of *Standards of Bibliographical Description,* by Curt F. Buhler, James G. McManaway, and Lawrence C. Wroth. In *College and Research Libraries* 11 # 4 (October, 1950): 399-401.

1951

51.	With Margaret E. Egan, eds. *Bibliographic Organization; Papers Presented Before the Fifteenth Annual Conference of the Graduate Library School, July 24-29, 1950.* Chicago: University of Chicago Press, 1951. Updated in *Wilson Library Bulletin* 40 # 8 (April, 1966): 703.
51.	"The Beginnings of Systematic Bibliography in America,

		1642-1799." In *Essays Honoring Lawrence C. Wroth*, ed. Frederick R. Goff. Portland, Maine: Anthoensen Press, 1951, 263-78.
51.		"Classification as the Basis of Bibliographic Organization." In *Bibliographic Organization*, eds. Jesse H. Shera and Margaret E. Egan, 72-93. Chicago: University of Chicago Press, 1951.
51.		*Report of the United States Delegate to the UNESCO Conference on the Improvement of Bibliographic Services, Paris, France, November 7-10, 1950.* Chicago: Graduate Library School, University of Chicago, 1951.
51.		With Margaret E. Egan. "The Training of Librarians and Documentalists in the United States." In *Enquiry Concerning the Professional Education of Librarians and Documentalists; Report to the Joint Committee of the International Federation of Library Associations and of the International Federation for Documentation*, by Suzanne Briet. Paris: UNESCO, 1951.
51	Jan.	"Bibliographic Management." *American Documentation* 2 # 1 (January, 1951): 47-54.
51	Jan.	With Margaret E. Egan. "Chicago Conference on Bibliographic Organization." *American Documentation* 2 (January, 1951): 5-7.
51	Jan.	"Documentation; its Scope and Limitations." *Library Quarterly* 21 # 1 (January, 1951): 13-26.
51	Jan.	Review of *A History of Libraries*, by Alfred Hessel. In *Library Quarterly* 21 # 1 (January, 1951): 46-48.
51	Feb.	With Margaret E. Egan. "The Present State of Bibliography in the United States; a Condensation of the U.S. Report on National and International Bibliographic Problems." *ALA Bulletin* 45 # 2 (February, 1951): 52 - 55.
51	Apr.	Review of *Catalogue of United States Census Publications, 1790-194:* by Henry J. Dubester. *In Library Quarterly* 21 # 2 (April, 1951*):* 144-45.
51	Apr 30.	"The UNESCO Conference on the Improvement of Bibliographic: Services." *U. S. Department of State Bulletin* 24 # 617 (April 30, 1951): 707-9.
51	Jul.	Review of *The H. W. ' Wilson Company*, by John Lawler. In *College and Research Libraries* 12 # 3 (July, 1951): 299-300.
51	Dec.	Review of *The Papers of Thomas Jefferson*, vols. 2-4, ed. Julian P. Boyd. In *Minnesota History* 32 # 4 (December, 1951): 248-49.

1952

52	Jan.	"Effect of Machine Methods on the Organization of Knowledge." *American Documentation* 3 # 1 (January, 1952): 15-20.
52	Jan.	Review of *Colon Classification*, 3d ed., by S. R. Ranganathan. In *Library Quarterly* 22 # 1 (January, 1952): 59-61.
52	Mar.	"The Preservation of Local Illinois Newspapers; a Report of the Committee on Local Illinois Newspapers." *ILA Record* 5 # 3 (March, 1952): 49-52.
52	Apr.	With Margaret E. Egan. "Foundations of *a* Theory of Bibliography *Library Quarterly* 22 # 2 (April, 1952): 125-37. Reprinted *Essays* on *Bibliography*, ed. Vito J. Brenni. Metuchen, N. J Scarecrow Press, 1975, 48-62.
52	Apr.	Review of *The Librarians' Conference of 1853*, by George B. Utley. *Library Quarterly* 22 # 2 (April, 1952): 145-47.
52	Oct.	"Special Librarianship and Documentation." *Library Trends* 1 # 2 (October, 1952, 1952): 189-99.
52	Oct.	Review of *The Fundamentals* of *Library Classification*, by Bernard I. Palmer and A. J. Wells. In *Library Quarterly* 22 # 4 (October, 1952): 354-56.
52	Dec.	"To the Alumni: Message of the Dean." News *Bulletin* [of the Alumni Association, School of Library Science, Western Reserve University] 49 (December, 1952): 1.

1953

53.		*Historians, Books, and Libraries.* **Cleveland: Press of Western Reserve University, 1953.**
53.		"Program for the Stimulation of National Bibliography in the Critical Areas." Chicago: American Library Association, 1953. Mimeographed.
53.		"Classification; Current Functions and Applications to the Subject Analysis of Library Materials." In *The Subject Analysis* of *Library Materials*, ed. Maurice F. Tauber, 29-42. New York: Columbia University School of Library Service, 1953.
53.		With Margaret E. Egan. "A Review of the Present State of Librarianship and Documentation. " In *Documentation*, by S. C. Bradford, 11-45. 2d ed. London: Crosby, Lockwood & Son, 1953.
53	Jan.	"Editorial." *American Documentation* 4 # 1 (January, 1953): ii.
53	Apr.	Review of *The Alexandrian Library*, by Edward A. Parsons. In *Library Quarterly* 23 # 2 (April, 1953): 137-38.
53	Jun.	Review of R. R. *Bowker, Militant Liberal*, by E. McClung Fleming. In *Mississippi Valley Historical Review* 40 # 1

		(June, 1953): 155-56.
53	Summer.	Review of *The Papers* of *Thomas Jefferson*, vols. 5 -6, ed. Julian P. Boyd. In *Minnesota History* 33 (Summer, 1953): 260-61.
53	Aug.	"Editorial." *American Documentation* 4 # 3 (August, 1953): 136.
53	Oct.	"Emergence of a New Institutional Structure for the Dissemination of Specialized Information." *American Documentation* 4 # 4 (October: 1953): 163-73. Also in *Communication* of *Specialized Information; Papers Presented Before the Seventeenth Annual Conference* of *the Graduate Library School* of *the University* of *Chicago, August 11-15, 1954*, ed. Margaret E. Egan, 113-28. Chicago: American Library Association, 1954.
52	Oct.	"Editorial." *American Documentation* 4 # 4 (October, 1953): ii.

1954

54	**Jan.**	**"Editorial."** ***American Documentation*** **5 # 1 (January, 1954): ii.**
54	Mar.	"Education for Librarianship; an Integrated Approach." *ALA Bulletin* 48 # 3 (March, 1954): 129-30, 169-73.
54	Apr.	Review of *Scholar's Workshop; Evolving Concepts* of *Library Service* by Kenneth J. Brough. In *College and Research Libraries* 15 # (April, 1954): 243 -44.
54	Apr.	"Editorial." *American Documentation* 5 # 2 (April, 1954): i.
54	Jul.	Review of *The Core of Education for Librarianship*, ed. Lester Asheim. In *College and Research Libraries* 15 # 3 (July, 1954): 348-52.
54	Jul.	Review of *Library Book Selection*, by S. R. Ranganathan. In *Library Quarterly* 24 # 3 (July, 1954): 255-57.
54	Jul.	Review of *Social Bibliography;* or *Physical Bibliography for Librarians*, by S. R. Ranganathan. In *Library Quarterly* 24 # 3(July, 1954), 255 - 57.
54	Jul.	Review of *Social Education Literature for Authors, Artists, Publishers, Teachers, Librarians, and Governments*, by S. R. Ranganathan. In *Library Quarterly* 24 # 3 (July, 1954): 255-57.
54	Aug.	"Editorial." *American Documentation* 5 # 3 (August, 1954): i.
54	Autumn.	Review of *The Papers of Thomas Jefferson*, vols. 7-8, ed. Julian P. Boyd. In *Minnesota History* 34 (Autumn, 1954): 118-19.
54	Oct.	"Editorial." *American Documentation* 5 # 4 (October, 1954): i.

1955

55. "Preface." In *Manual for Use in the Cataloging of Audio-visual Materials for a High School Library*, by Eunice Keen, iii. Lakeland, Fla.: The Author, 1955.

55 Jan. "Editorial: Ralph Albert Beals" and "Jack Cassius Morris." *American Documentation* 6 # 1 (January, 1955): ii.

55 Mar. Review of *The University of Virginia Library, 1825 -1 950: Story of a Jefferson Foundation*, by Harry Clemons. In *Mississippi Valley Historical Review* 41 # 4 (March, 1955): 722 - 23.

55 Apr. "The Role of the College Library: a Reappraisal." In *Library - Instructional Integration on the College Level*. ACRL Monographs, No. 13, April, 1955, 6 -13. Chicago: Association of College and Research Libraries, 1955.

55 Apr. Review of *The Technical Report*, ed. B. H. Weil. In *American Documentation* 6 # 2 (April, 1955): 104 - 5.

55 Apr. "Editorial: The Truth, the Whole Truth..." *American Documentation* 6 # 2 (April, 1955): ii.

55 Summer. Review of *The Papers of Thomas Jefferson*, vols. 9-10, ed. Julian P. Boyd. In *Minnesota History* 34 (Summer, 1955): 252-53.

55 Jul. With Barbara Denison. "Preliminary Planning Conference on Information Processing and Correlation. " *American Documentation* 6 # 3 (July, 1955): 162-66.

55 Jul. "Editorial: A House Divided." *American Documentation* 6 # 3 (July, 1955): ii.

55 Oct. Review of *Standards* in *the Domain of Documentation*, issued by Technical Committee 46--Documentation, International Organization for Standardization. In *Journal of Cataloging and Classification* 11 # 4 (October, 1955): 252-54.

55 Oct. "Editorial: Toward the Formation of a Library Editors' Council." *American Documentation* 6 # 4 (October, 1955): ii.

1956

56. With Margaret E. Egan. *The Classified Catalog; Basic Principles and Practices*. **Chicago: American Library Association, 1956.**

56. With Allen Kent and James W. Perry, eds. *Documentation in Action*. New York: Reinhold, 1956.

56. "Areas for Research. " In *Documentation* in *Action*, eds. Jesse

		H. Shera, Allen Kent, and James W. Perry, 447-58. New York: Reinhold, 1956.
56.		"Foreword." In *Machine Literature Searching*, eds. James W. Perry, Allen Kent, and Madeline M. Berry, v-vi. New York: Press of Western Reserve University and Interscience, 1956.
56.		"In the Beginning was the Word." In *Documentation in Action*, eds. Jesse H. Shera, Allen Kent, and James W. Perry, 1-11. New York: Reinhold, 1956.
56.		"Program for Education of Librarians and Documentalists of the Future. " In *Documentation in Action*, eds. Jesse H. Shera, Allen Kent, and James W. Perry, 307-12. New York: Reinhold, 1956.
56	Jan.	"Training the Chemical Librarian; a Challenge and an Opportunity." *Special Libraries* 47 # 1 (January, 1956): 8-16.
56	Jan.	Abstract of "Training the Chemical Librarian; a Challenge and, Opportunity." *News Letter of the American Association of Library Schools* 7 (January, 1956): 11-13.
56	Jan.	"Editorial." *American Documentation* 7 # 1 (January, 1956): ii.
56	Feb.	"Librarianship in a High Key." *ALA Bulletin* 50 # 2 (February, 1956): 103-5.
56	Spring.	"Research and Training in Documentation at Western Reserve University, " *Microcosm* 2 # 1 (Spring, 1956): 3.
56	Apr.	With Barbara Denison. "Documentation in Action." *American Scientist* 44 # 2 (April, 1956): 94a-104a.
56	Apr.	"Mirror for Documentalists." *District of Columbia Libraries* 27 # (April, 1956): 2-4.
56	Apr.	Review of *The University Library*, by Louis Round Wilson and Maurice F. Tauber. In *American Documentation* 7 # 2 (April, 1956): 137.
56	Apr.	"Editorial: Needed--'Creative Documentation.'" *American Documentation* 7 # 2 (April, 1956): ii.
56	Jul.	"On the Teaching of Cataloging. " *Journal of Cataloging and Classification* 12 # 3 (July, 1956): 130-32.
56	Jul.	"Editorial: Fundamental Research; a Few Fundamentals. " *American Documentation* 7 # 3 (July, 1956), ii.
56	Jul-Aug.	"Report of the Publications Committee." *Special Libraries* 47 # 6 (July-August, 1956): 280-274.
56	Sep.	"Putting Knowledge to Work; the Reaffirmation of a credo, a Rededication to the Faith." *Special Libraries* 47 # 7 (September, 1956): 322-26.
56	Sep.	Review of *The Boston Public Library; a Centennial History*, by Walter Muir Whitehill. In *Mississippi Valley Historical*

		Review 42 # 2 (September, 1956): 339-40.
56	Sep.	Review of *The Papers of Thomas Jefferson*, vols. 11 -12, ed. Julian P. Boyd. In *Minnesota History* 35 (September, 1956): 144-45.
56	Oct.	"Editorial: UNESCO--Ten Years After." *American Documentation* 7 # 4 (October, 1956): ii.
56	Nov.	"Biographical Notes: L. S. Dutton; E. W. King." *College and Research Libraries* 17 (November, 1956): 512-14.
56	Dec 1.	"Knowledge Goes Berserk." *Saturday Review* 39 (December 1, 1956): 69- 71.

<u>1957</u>

57.		**With Allen Kent and James W. Perry, eds. *Information Systems in Documentation*. Advances in Documentation and Library Science, vol. 2. New York: Interscience, 1957.**
57.		"Foreword." In *Documentation and Information Retrieval*, by James W. Perry and Allen Kent, iii-iv. Cleveland: Press of Western Reserve University and Interscience, 1957.
57.		"Pattern, Structure, and Conceptualization in Classification." In *Proceedings of the International Study Conference on Classification in Information Retrieval, Dorking, 1957*, 15 - 27. London: ASLIB, 1957.
57.		Review of "Selection." Chap. 7 in the *FID Manual of Document Reproduction and Selection*. In *Review of Documentation* 24 # 3 (1957): 121.
57	Jan.	"Biographical Sketch: Russell S. Dozer." *College and Research Libraries* 18 (January, 1957): 45.
57	Jan.	Review of *Essays in the History of Ideas*, by Arthur O. Lovejoy. In *College and Research Libraries* 18 # 1 (January, 1957): 82-84.
57	Jan.	Review of *Man on his Past*, by Herbert Butterfield. In *College and Research Libraries* 18 # I (January, 19 57): 82-84.
57	Jan.	"Editorial: Loue par Ceux-ci..." *American Documentation* 8 # 1 (January, 1957): ii.
57	Jan 1.	"The Librarians' New Frontier." *Library Journal* 82 #1 (January 1, 1957): 26-28.
57	Apr.	"Editorial: Thoughts on New Year's Eve." *American Documentation* 8 # 2 (April, 1957): ii.
57	Jun.	Review of *The Papers of Thomas Jefferson*, vol. 13, ed. Julian P. Boyd. In *Minnesota History* 35 (June, 1957): 285-86.
57	Jul.	"Editorial." *American Documentation* 8 # 3 (July, 1957): ii.
57	Oct.	"Research and Development in Documentation." *Library Trends* 6 # 2 (October, 1957): 187-206.

57	Oct.	"Editorial: Horne Thoughts from Abroad." *American Documentation* 8 # 4 (October, 1957): ii.
57	Dec.	Review of *Imprints on History; Book Publishers and American Frontiers,* by Madeline B. Stern. In *Mississippi Valley Historical Review* 44 # 3 (December, 1957): 576-77.

1958

58.		**With Allen Kent and James W. Perry, eds. *Information Resources; a Challenge to American Science and Industry.* Cleveland: Press of Western Reserve University, 1958.**
58.		With Allen Kent. *Resolution of the Literature Crisis in the Decade 1960-1970.* Cleveland: Center for Documentation and Communication Research, School of Library Science, Western Reserve University, 1958.
58	Winter.	With Margaret E. Egan. "Comment" [on Osborn's Review of *The Classified Catalog*]. *Library Resources and Technical Services* 2 (Winter, 1958): 55.
58	Jan.	"Classification at Dorking; the International Study Conference on Classification for Information Retrieval." *Library Resources and Technical Services* 2 # 1 (January, 1958): 33-43.
58	Jan.	"Editorial: Of Mountains, and Coffee, and Documentation." *American Documentation* 9 # 1 (January, 1958): ii.
58	Apr.	"Editorial: Librarians and the Sputnik. " *American Documentation* 9 # 2 (April, 1958): ii.
58	Jun.	"Background Courses in Education for Librarianship." *Association of American Library Schools Bulletin,* June, 1958, 20-22.
58	Jul.	"Editorial: The Parlement of Foules." *American Documentation* 9 # 3 (July, 1958): ii.
58	Oct.	"Education for Documentation." *Special Libraries* 49 # 8 (October, 1958): 389-90.
58	Oct.	"Editorial: The New World's Debt to the Old." *American Documentation* 9 # 4 (October, 1958): ii.

1959

59.		**"What Lies Ahead in Classification." In *The Role of Classification in the Modern American Library,* eds. Thelma Eaton and Donald E. Strout, 116-28. Champaign, Ill.: Illini Union Bookstore, 1959.**

59	Jan-Feb.	"The Place of Bookbinding in the Library School Curriculum." *Rub-Off 10 # 1 (January-February*, 1959): 1-3.
59	Jan.	"Editorial: Antidote for Tranquilizers." *American Documentation* 10 # 1 (January, 1959): ii.
59	Apr.	"In Memoriam: Margaret E. Egan." *Ohio Library Association Bulletin* 29 (April, 1959): 27.
59	Apr.	"Isis and the Librarian's Quest for Unity." *Ohio Library Association Bulletin* 29 # 2 (April, 1959): 19, 21.
59	Apr.	"Editorial: The Renaissance of Classification." *American Documentation* 10 # 2 (April, 1959): ii.
59	Jun.	Review of *The Papers of Thomas Jefferson*, vols. 14-15, ed. Julian P. Boyd. In *Minnesota History* 36 (June, 1959): 231-32.
	Jun 1.	"Not Novel but Bears Repeating." [Comment elicited from Betty Bacon, "My Year in Library School; Some Second Thoughts."]" *Library Journal* 84 # 11 (June 1, 1959): 1746. See ibid., 83 : 1741-52, for the context in which Shera's remarks occur.
59	Jul.	"Editorial: A Science Full of Living Problems. " *American Documentation* 10 # 3 (July, 1959): ii.
59	Oct.	"New Tools for Easing the Burden of Historical Research." *American Documentation* 10 # 4 (October, 1959): 274-77.
59	Oct.	"Editorial: The Historian and Documentation." *American Documentation* 10 # 4 (October, 1959): ii.
59	Nov 1.	"Standardizing Language for Machine Searching." *Library Journal* 84, (November 1, 1959): 3386.

<u>1960</u>

60. "Communicating Office of Education Statistics." In *Report,* by U. S. Office of Education, Advisory Committee of Users of Educational Statistics, 33-41. Washington, D. C.: U. S. Department of Health, Education and Welfare, 1960.

60. "Present Day Methods for the Storage and Retrieval of Information." In *Proceedings of a Work Conference on Bibliographic Control of Newer Educational Media*, eds. Margaret I. Rufsvold and Carolyn Guss, 42-55. Bloomington, Indiana: Indiana University, 1960.

60. "What Lies Ahead in Classification." In *The Role of Classification in the Modern American Library*, eds. Thelma Eaton and Donald E. Strout, 116-28. Champaign, Ill.: Illini Union Bookstore, 1960. Also in *Libraries and the Organization of Knowledge*, ed. D. J. Foskett, 129-42. Hamden, Conn.: Archon Books, 1965.

60.		"Social Epistemology, General Semantics, and Libraries." *Yearbook of the Institute of General Semantics,* nos. 26- 27 (1960): 19-21. Also in *Wilson Library Bulletin* 35 # 10 (June, 1961): 767-70; and in *Libraries and the Organization of Knowledge,* ed. D. J. Foskett, 12-17. Hamden, Conn.: Archon Books, 1965.
60	Jan.	Review of *The Making of an American Community,* by Merle Curti et al. In *Ohio Historical Quarterly* 69 # 1 (January, 1960): 86-89.
60	Jan.	Review of *A Passion for Books,* by Lawrence C. Powell. In *Bulletin of the Ohio Library Association* 30 # 1 (January, 1960): 6-7.
60	Jan.	"Editorial: The Solitary Esophagus." *American Documentation* 11 (January, 1960): ii.
60	Apr.	"Shivali Ramamrita Ranganathan." *American Documentation* 11 (April, 1960): 89-90.
60	Apr.	"Editorial: A New High at Lehigh." *American Documentation* 11 (April, 1960): ii.
60	May 1.	"Theory and Technique in Library Education." *Library Journal* 85 # 9 (May 1, 1960): 1736-39. Also in *Libraries and the Organization of Knowledge,* ed. D. J. Foskett, 174-77. Hamden, Conn.: Archon Books, 1965. Abstracted in *Library Science Abstracts* 11 (1960): 101 # 10128.
60	Oct.	"Editorial: A Mandate for Documentation." *American Documentation* 11 (October, 1960): ii.
60	Nov.	"The Changing Philosophy of Bibliographic Classification." *Revue de la Documentation* 27 # 4 (November, 1960): 139 -40.

1961

61.		**"Automation Without Fear." In** ***The Sayers Memorial Volume: Essays in Librarianship in Memory of William Charles Berwick Sayers,*** **eds. D. J. Foskett and B. I. Palmer, 168-81. London: The Library Association, 1961. Also in** ***ALA Bulletin*** **55 # 9 (October, 1961): 787-94; and in** ***Documentation and the Organization of Knowledge,*** **ed. D. J. Foskett, 84-96. Hamden, Conn.: Archon Books, 1966.**
61.		"Common Languages in Librarianship and Documentation." In *Information Retrieval and Machine Translation,* Pt. II, ed. Allen Kent, 1051-60. New York: Interscience Publishers, 1961. Also in *Documentation and the Organization of Knowledge,* ed. D. J. Foskett, 134-

61.		46. Hamden, Conn.: Archon Books, 1966. "Developments in Machine Literature Searching." In *The Clarification, Unification, and Integration of Information Storage and Retrieval,* eds. Edward A. Tomeski, Richard W. Westcott, and Mary Covington, 22-34. Proceedings of February 23, 1961 Symposium. New York: Special Libraries Association, 1961. Also in *Documentation and the Organization of Knowledge,* ed. D. J. Foskett, 97-107. Hamden, Conn.: Archon Books, 1966.
61.		"Objectives of the School of Library Science." In *Western Reserve University, School of Library Science, Academic Year 1961-62,* 1-5. Cleveland: Western Reserve University, School of Library Science, 1961.
61	Winter.	"An Educational Program for Special Librarians." *Journal of Education for Librarianship 1 # 3 (Winter, 1961): 121- 28.* Also in *Libraries and the Organization of Knowledge,* ed. D. J. Foskett, 178-84. Hamden, Conn.: Archon Books, 1965. Abstracted in *Library Science Abstracts* 12 (1961): 95 # 11126.
61	Jan.	Review of *Borrowings from the Bristol Library, 1773-1874,* by Paul Kaufman. In *College and Research Libraries* 22 # 1 (January, 1961): 80-82.
61	Spring.	Review of *Cataloging and Classification,* by Maurice F. Tauber. In *Library Resources and Technical Services* 5 # 2 (Spring, 1961): 162-63.
61	Spring.	Review of *Subject Headings,* by Carlyle J. Frarey. In *Library Resources and Technical Services* 5 (Spring, 1961): 162 -63.
61	Jun.	"Social Epistemology, General Semantics, and Libraries." *Wilson Library Bulletin* 35 # 10 (June, 1961): 767-770. Also in *Yearbook of the Institute of General Semantics* # 26-27 (1960): 19 - 21; and in *Libraries and the Organization of Knowledge,* ed. D. J. Foskett, 12-17. Hamden, Conn.: Archon Books, 1965. Abstracted in *Library Science Abstracts* 12 (1961): 267 # 11588.
61	Jun 15.	"The Librarian and the Machine." *Library Journal* 86 # 12 (June 15, 1961): 2250- 54. Abstracted in *Library Science Abstracts* 12 (1961): 250 # 11555.
61	Aug.	"How Much is a Physicist's Inertia Worth?" *Physics Today* 14 # (August, 1961): 42-63. Reprinted in *Reader in the Academic Library,* ed. Michael M. Reynolds, 190-92. Washington, D. C.: NCR Microcard Editions, 1969.
61	Sep.	"Cloudland Revisited." *Wilson Library Bulletin* 36 (September 1961): 69. Also in *The Compleat Librarian,* 3-4. Cleveland: Press of Case Western Reserve University, 1971.

61	Oct.	"Automation Without Fear." ALA *Bulletin* 55 # 9 (October, 1961): 787-94. Also in *The Sayers Memorial Volume; Essays in Librarianship in Memory of William Charles Berwick Sayers*, eds. D. J. Foskett and B. I. Palmer, 168- 81. London: Library Association, 1~61); and in *Documentation and the Organization of Knowledge*, ed. D. J. Foskett, 84-96. Hamden, Conn.: Archon Books, 1966. Abstracted in *Library Science Abstracts* 12 (1961): 335 # 11781.
61	Oct.	"Of Red Carpets and Pruning Shears." *Wilson Library Bulletin* 36 (October, 1961): 170, 175. Also in *The Compleat Librarian*, 5-7. Cleveland: Press of Case Western Reserve University, 1971.
61	Fall.	"What is Librarianship?" *Louisiana Library Association Bulletin* 21 # 36 (Fall, 1961): 95-97. Reprinted in *American Library Philosophy*, ed. Barbara McCrimmon, 165 - 71. Hamden, Conn.: Shoestring Press, 1975.
61	Nov.	"Cult of the Audio-visual." *Wilson Library Bulletin* 36 (November, 1961): 251.
61	Dec.	"A Curriculum for Mr. Ciardi." *Wilson Library Bulletin* 36 (December, 1961): 330.

1962

62.		**With Barbara Denison. "College and University Libraries." In *Encyclopedia Americana* 17: 385-88. New York: Americana Corporation, 1962). Contained in article entitled "Libraries."**
62.		"How Engineers Can Keep Abreast of Professional and Technical Literature." *ASME Design Engineering Conference*, 49-53. Chicago: American Society of Mechanical Engineers, 1962. Also in *Documentation and the Organization of Knowledge*, ed. D. J. Foskett, 147-57. Hamden, Conn.: Archon Books, 1966.
62.	Jan.	"The Dignity and Advancement of Bacon." *College and Research Libraries* 23 #1 (January, 1962): 18-23. Also in *Libraries and the Organization of Knowledge*, ed. D. J. Foskett, 143-50. Hamden, Conn. Archon Books, 1965.
62	Jan.	"The 'Dismal Science' and Librarianship." *Wilson Library Bulletin* 36 (January, 1962): 382. Also in *The Compleat Librarian*, 8-10. Cleveland: Press of Case Western Reserve University, 1971.
62	Jan.	Review of *Index Mechanization Project, July 1, 1958-June 30, 1960*, by the National Library of Medicine. In *Library Quarterly 32* # 1 (January, 1962): 85 - 86.

62	Feb.	"Officer, Arrest That Book!" *Wilson Library Bulletin* 36 (February, 1962): 488. Also in *The Compleat Librarian*, 11-l3. Cleveland: Press of Case Western Reserve University, 1971.
62	Mar.	"Cards is Cards." *Wilson Library Bulletin* 36 (March, 1962): 586, 588.
62	Mar-Apr.	"On Keeping Up with Keeping Up." *UNESCO Bulletin for Libraries* 16 # 2 (March-April, 1962): 64-72. Also in *Documentation and the Organization of Knowledge*, ed. D. J. Foskett, 72-83. Hamden, Conn.: Archon Books, 1966.
62	Apr.	"The Bad-Humor Man." *Wilson Library Bulletin* 36 (April, 1962): 682, Also in *The Compleat Librarian*, 14-16. Cleveland: Press of Case Western Reserve University, 1971.
62	May.	"On the Permanence of the Invisible." *Wilson Library Bulletin 36* (May, 1962): 764. Also in *The Compleat Librarian, 17-19*. Cleveland: Press of Case Western Reserve University, 1971.
62	Summer.	"The Book Catalog and the Scholar; a RE-examination of an Old Partnership." *Library Resources and Technical Services* 6 # 3 (Summer, 1962): 210-16. Also in *Book Catalogs*, by Robert E. Kingery and Maurice F. Tauber, 1-12. New York: Scarecrow, 1963; and in *Libraries and the Organization of Knowledge*, ed. D. J. Foskett, 151-57. Hamden, Conn.: Archon Books, 1965.
62	Jun.	"Only Low Conversation." *Wilson Library Bulletin* 36 (June, 1962): 846.
62	Jun.	Review of *The Papers of Thomas Jefferson*, vol. 16, ed. Julian P. Boyd. In *Minnesota History* 42 (June, 1962): 90-91.
62	Jul.	Review of *Research Opportunities in American Cultural History*, ed. John Francis McDermott. In *Library Quarterly* 32 # 3 (July, 1962): 236-38.
62	Sep.	"Fremont Rides Through the Dewey, Dewey Fog." *Wilson Library Bulletin* 37 (September, 1962): 69-72, 81.
62	Sep.	Review of *Rider's International Classification for the Arrangement of Books on the Shelves of General Libraries*, by Fremont Rider. In *Wilson Library Bulletin* 37 (September, 1962): 69-72.
62	Oct.	"What is a Book That a Man May Know it?" *Wilson Library Bulletin* 37 (October, 1962): 176. Also in *The Compleat Librarian, 20-22*. Cleveland: Press of Case Western Reserve University, 1971.
62	Oct.	Review of *The Western Book Trade; Cincinnati as a Nineteenth Century Publishing and Book Trade Center*, by Walter Sutton. In *Ohio History* 71 # 3 (October, 1962): 267-69.

62	Nov-Dec.	"S. R. Ranganathan; One American View." *Pakistan Library Review* 4 # 3-4 (November-December, 1962): 6-8. Also in *Wilson Library Bulletin* 37 (March, 1963): 581-82; and in the Indian journal *Herald of Library Science* 2 # 4 (1963): 210-l3. Abstracted in *Library Science Abstracts* 15 (1964): 186 # 14376.
62	Nov.	"Discipline, Dissent, and Documentation. " *Wilson. Library Bulletin* 37 (November, 1962): 290 -91.
62	Dec.	"Yes, Virginia, There is a Verner Clapp." *Wilson Library Bulletin* 37 (December, 1962): 358-59. Also in *The Compleat Librarian*, 23-25. Cleveland: Press of Case Western University, 1971.
62	Dec.	"Little Girls Don't Play Librarian." *Library Journal* 87 # 22 (December 15, 1962): 4483-87. Abstracted in *Library Science Abstracts* 14 (1963): 9 # 12835.

1963

63. **"The Book Catalog and the Scholar; a Re - examination of an Old Partnership. " In *Book Catalogs*, by Robert E. Kingery and Maurice F. Tauber, 1-12. New York: Scarecrow, 1963. Also in *Library Resources* and *Technical Services* 6 # 3 (Summer, 1962): 210 - 16); and *Libraries and the Organization of Knowledge,* ed. D. J. Foskett, 151- 57. Hamden, Conn.: Archon Books, 1965.**

63. "The Propaedeutic of the New Librarianship." In *Information Retrieval Today: Papers Presented at the Institute Conducted by the Library School and the Center for Continuation Study, University of Minnesota, September 19-22, 1962,* ed. Wesley Simonton, 5-19. Minneapolis: Center for Continuation Study, University of Minnesota, 1963. Also in *Documentation and the Organization of Knowledge*, ed. D. J. Foskett, 54-71. Hamden, Conn: Archon Books, 1966.

63. "Staffing Library Services to Meet Student Needs -- Library Education." In *Student Use of Libraries; an Inquiry into the Needs of Students, Libraries, and the Educational Process,* by the American Library Association, 1-7. Chicago: American Library Association, 1963. Also in *Student Use of Libraries* . . . , by the American Library Association, 122-33. Chicago: America Library Association, 1964; and *Libraries and the Organization of Knowledge,* ed. D. J. Foskett, 197-207. Hamden, Conn.: Archon Books, 1965.

63	Jan.	"Bibliotecas del Mañana." *El Correo* 16 (January, 1963): 11-13.
63	Jan.	"Die Bibliothek von Morgen." *Kurier* 16 (January, 1963): 8-11.
63	Jan.	"Bibliotheque de la Demain. 11 Le *Courrier* 16 (January, 1963): 11-13.
63	Jan.	In Defense of Miss Groby." *Wilson Library Bulletin* 37 (January, 1963): 430. Also in *The Compleat Librarian, 26-28.* Cleveland: Press of Case Western Reserve University, 1971.
63	Jan.	"The Library of the Future. " *UNESCO Courier* 16 (January, 1963): 11-13. Translated into French, Spanish, German, Russian, Japanese, and Portuguese. Also in *Indian Librarian* 18 (June, 1963): 20-24. Abstracted (1963): 294 # 13580.
63	Jan 1.	"Formulate a Professional Philosophy." *Library Journal* 88 (January 1, 1963): 50. For the context of these remarks see ibid., 39 -50.
63	Feb.	"Libraries are for Growing." *Wilson Library Bulletin* 37 (February, 1963): 498-99. Also in *The Compleat Librarian,* 29-31. Cleveland: Press of Case Western Reserve University, 1971.
63	Feb 1.	Review of *Scientific Books, Libraries, and Collections,* by John L. Thornton and R. 1. J. Tully. In *Library Journal* 88 # 3 (February 1, 1963): 547-48.
63	Mar.	"S. R. Ranganathan; One American View." *Wilson Library Bulletin* 37 (March, 1963): 581-82. Also in *Pakistan Library Review* 4 # 3-4 (November-December, 1962): 6-8; and in *Herald of Library Science* 2 # 4 (1963): 210-13.
63	Mar-Apr.	"Toward a Program for Ohio Librarians." *The Rub-Off* 14 # 2 (March-April, 1963): 1-3.
63	Apr.	"D.R.S. to the G.L.S." *Wilson Library Bulletin* 37 (April, 1963): 687, 715.
63	Apr.	"Toward a New Dimension for Library Education." *ALA Bulletin* 57 # 4 (April, 1963): 313-17. Also in *Libraries and the Organization of Knowledge,* ed. D. J. Foskett, 161-67. Hamden, Conn.: Archon Books, 1965.
63	May.	"Bibliotecas del Mañana." *Decisiones Gerenciales* y *Computadoras* 5-6 (May, 1963): 22-26.
63	May.	"A Book for Burning." *Wilson Library Bulletin* 37 (May, 1963): 790. Also in *The Compleat Librarian,* 32-34. Cleveland: Press of Case Western Reserve University, 1971.

63	Jun.	"Bamboo and Silk and the Art of Talking Back." *Wilson Library Bulletin* 37 (June, 1963): 870. Also in *The Compleat Librarian*, 35-37. Cleveland: Press of Case Western Reserve University, 1971.
63	Jun.	"Library of the Future." *Indian Librarian* 18 (June, 1963): 20-24. Also in *UNESCO Courier* 16 (January, 1963): 11-13.
63	Jun.	Review of *The Scarlet Letter*, by Nathaniel Hawthorne. In *American Notes and Queries* 1 # 10 (June, 1963): 159-60.
63	Jul.	Review of *Itself an Education*, by Bernard I. Palmer. In *Library Quarterly* 33 # 3 (July, 1963): 289-91.
63	Jul 1.	Review of *Enlarged Prints from Library Microfilms*, by William M. Hawken. In *Library Journal* 88 # 13 (July 1, 1963): 2670.
63	Sep.	"Far Above Cayuga's Waters." *Wilson Library Bulletin 38* (September, 1963): 73, 93.
63	Sep.	Review of *Directory of Special Libraries and Information Centers*, comp. Anthony T. Kruzas. In *Library Journal* 88 # 16 (September, 1963): 3194 -95.
63	Sep 15.	Review of *Nonconventional Technical Information Retrieval Systems in Current Use*, by the National Science Foundation. In *College and Research Libraries* 24 # 5 (September 15, 1963): 435-37.
63	Oct.	"S. R. Ranganathan; a Study." *Herald of Library Science* 2 (October, 1963): 210-13.
63	Oct.	"Where is Today's Brother Keppel'?" *Wilson Library Bulletin* 38 (October, 1963): 185, 190. Also in *The Compleat Librarian*, 38-40. Cleveland: Press of Case Western Reserve University, 1971.
63	Nov.	"The 'Guide' Stands First." *Wilson Library Bulletin* 38 (October, 1963): 285, 295. Also in *The Compleat Librarian*, 38-40. Cleveland: Press of Case Western Reserve University, 971.
	Nov 1.	"O! Medium, O! Media." *Library Journal* 88 # 19 (November 1, 1963): 4149-51. Also in *The Compleat Librarian*, 160-66. Cleveland: Press of Case Western Reserve University, 1971.
63	Dec.	"Trusteeship--Trust or Bust?" *Wilson Library Bulletin* 38 (December, 1963): 354, 356. Also in *The Compleat Librarian*, 44-46. Cleveland: Press of Case Western Reserve University, 971.
63	Dec 1.	Review of *Charles Evans, American Bibliographer*, by Edward G. Holley. In *Library Journal* 88 #21 (December, 1963): 4614.

1964

64?		With Margaret E. Egan. *Examen del Estado Actuel de la Biblioteconomia y de la Documentacion*. Serie A: Bibliotecologia y Documentacion; Estudios y Trabajos, 2. Santa Fe, Argentina: Centro de Documentacion e Informacion de Asuntos Municipales Doctor Alcides Greca, [1965]. Translated from "Introduction" to *Documentation*, by S. C. Bradford. 2nd ed. London: C. Lockwood, 1953.
64.		"Librarianship as a Career." In *World Topics Yearbook*, 207-17. Lake Bluff, Ill: United Educators, 1965.
64.		"Libraries, History of." In *Encyclopedia International* 10:521-22. New York: Grolier, 1964.
64.		With Barbara Denison. "Library." In *American Educators Encyclopedia*, 9:L124-L151. Lake Bluff, Ill.: United Educators, 1964.
64.		"Ohio Library Association. Notes on State Library Association Activities, 1963-1964." Grolier Incorporated. New York. 1964.
64.		"Staffing Library Service to Meet Student Needs--Library Education." In *Student Use of Libraries; an Inquiry into the Needs of Students, Libraries, and the Educational Process*, by the American Library Association, 122-33. Papers of the Conference Within a Conference, July 16-18, 1963. Chicago: American Library Association, 1964. Also published as a separate in 1963; and in *Libraries and the Organization of Knowledge*, ed. D. J. Foskett, 197-207. Hamden, Conn.: Archon Books, 1965.
64.	Winter.	"In Defense of Diversity." *Journal of Education for Librarianship* 4 # 3 (Winter, 1964): 137-42.
64	Winter.	"Western Reserve University Library School." *Ohioana; of Ohio and Ohioans* 7 # 4 (Winter, 1964): 131-33.
64	Jan.	"From the President." *Ohio Library Association Bulletin* 34 (January, 1964): 1-2.
64	Jan.	"Walter Brahm Appointed State Librarian of Connecticut." *Ohio Library Association Bulletin* 34 (January, 1964): 3.
64	Jan.	"A Warm Puppy is not Happiness. " *Wilson Library Bulletin* 38 (January, 1964): 409. Also in *The Compleat Librarian*, 47-49. Cleveland: Press of Case Western Reserve University, 1971.
64	Jan.	"Year for Action." *Ohio Library Association Bulletin* 34 (January, 1964): 1-2.
64	Feb.	"The Epistle of Paul to the Pedants." *Wilson Library Bulletin* 38 (February, 1964): 485. Also in *The Compleat*

		Librarian, 50-52. Cleveland: Press of Case Western Reserve University, 1971.
64	Feb.	Review of *Classification and Indexing in the Social Sciences,* by D. J. Foskett. In *Revue Internationale de Documentation* 31 # 1 (February, 1964): 31-32.
64	Feb.	Review of *Readings in Special Librarianship,* by Harold S. Sharp. In *Special Libraries* 44 # 2 (February, 1964): 121-22.
64	Spring.	Review of *William Frederick Poole and the Modern Library Movement,* by William L. Williamson. In *Wisconsin Magazine of History* 47 # 3 (Spring, 1964): 272-73.
64	Mar.	"Backward to Normalcy." *Wilson Library Bulletin* 38 (March, 1964): 561.
64	Apr.	"From the President." *Ohio Library Association Bulletin* 34 (April, 1964), 1-2.
64	Apr.	"Wheels Begin to Turn." *Ohio Library Association Bulletin* 34 (April, 1964): 1-2.
64	Apr.	"William to Tucker to Jess. " *Wilson Library Bulletin* 38 (April, 1964): 677. Also in *The Compleat Librarian,* 53-55. Cleveland: Press of Case Western Reserve University, 1971.
64	May.	"Introduction" [to a special issue on documentation and automation]. *Wilson Library Bulletin* 38 # 9 (May, 1964): 741-42.
64	May.	"Of Librarians and Other Aborigines." *Wilson Library Bulletin* 38 (May, 1964): 781.
64	May 1.	Review of *The Printed Book Catalog in American Libraries, 1723-1900,* by Joseph Ranz. In *Library Journal* 89 # 11 (May 1,1964): 1940 -41.
64	Jun.	"The Compleat Librarian." *Wilson Library Bulletin* 38 (June, 1964): 867, 878. Also in *The Compleat Librarian,* 56-59. Cleveland: Press of Case Western Reserve University, 1971.
64	Jun.	"Dimensions of the Master's Program." *ALA Bulletin* 35 # 6 (June, 1964): 519-22. Also in *Libraries and the Organization of Knowledge,* ed. D. J. Foskett, 168 - 73. Hamden, Conn.: Archon Books, 1965.
64	Jul.	Report to the Committee on Guidelines for Medical School Libraries of the Association of American Medical Colleges on *The Future of the Medical School Library.* July, 1964.
64	Jul.	"Automation and the Reference Librarian." *RQ* 3 # 6 (July, 1964): 3-7. Also in *Documentation and the Organization of Knowledge,* ed. D. J. Foskett, 158- 68. Hamden, Conn.: Archon Books, 1966.
64	Jul.	"Darwin, Bacon, and Research in Librarianship. " *Library*

		Trends 13 # 1 (July, 1964): 141 - 4 9. Also in *Libraries and the Organization of Knowledge,* ed. D. J. Foskett, 208-216.Hamden, Conn.: Archon Books, 1965. Abstracted in *Library Science Abstracts* 16 (1965): 216 # 1 5504.
64	Jul.	"From the President." *Ohio Library Association Bulletin* 34 (July, 1964): 1-2.
64	Jul.	Review of *Henry Stevens of Vermont: American Rare Book Dealer in London, 1845-1886,* by Wyman Parker. In *Library Quarterly* 34 # 3 (July, 1964): 272-73.
64	Sep.	"The Turning of the Worm." *Wilson Library Bulletin* 39 (September, 1964): 73, 84.
64	Oct.	"From the President." *Ohio Library Association Bulletin* 34 (October, 1964): 1-2.
64	Oct.	"On the Encouragement of Reading." *Wilson Library Bulletin* 39 (October, 1964): 169, 191. Also in *The Compleat Librarian,* 60-62. Cleveland: Press of Case Western Reserve University, 1971.
64	Nov.	"The Future, Too, is Prologue." *Wilson Library Bulletin* 39 (November, 1964): 253, 280.
64	Nov.	"The Library of the Future; a WLB Symposium." *Wilson Library Bulletin* 39 # 3 (November, 1964): 228-43. Abstracted in *Library and Science Abstracts* 15 (1964): 282 # 14640.
64	Dec.	"Daedalus, Icarus, and the Technological Revolution." *Wilson Library Bulletin* 39 (December, 1964): 335. Also in *The Compleat Librarian,* 63-65. Cleveland: Press of Case Western Reserve University, 1971.
64	Dec.	Review of *Some Problems of a General Classification Scheme,* (Report of a Conference Held in London, June 1963), by the Library Association. In *Journal of Documentation* 20 (December, 1964): 238-40.

1965

65.	***Libraries and the Organization of Knowledge,* ed. D. J. Foskett. Hamden, Conn.: Archon Books, 1965.**
65.	"Changing Concepts of Classification; Philosophical and Educational Implications. " In *Library Science Today: Ranganathan Festschrift,* ed. P. N. Kaula, 1:37 - 48. New York: Asia Publishing House, 1965.
65.	"Introduction and Welcome." In *The Education of Science Information Personnel,* eds. A. J. Goldwyn and Alan M. Rees, 1-5. Proceedings of an Invitational Conference, 1964. Cleveland: Center for Documentation and Communication Research, School of Library Science, Western Reserve University, 1965.

65.		"The Problem of Finance; Working Paper No. 4." In *Problems of Library School Administration,* ed. Sarah R. Reed, 33-45. Report of an Institute, April 14-15, 1965. Washington, D. C.: U. S. Department of Health, Education and Welfare, Office of Education, 1965.
65.		With Theodore C. Hines. "Report of Consultants to the Ad Hoc Committee on the Establishment of a School of Library Studies at the State University of New York a t Buffalo." Buffalo, N. Y.: Stat e University of New York at Buffalo, 1965. Mimeographed. 51p.
65.		"The Ag of Paradox." *Wilson Library Bulletin* 39 (January, 1965): 409, 414. Also in *The Compleat Librarian,* 66-68. Cleveland: Press of Case Western Reserve University, 1971.
65.		"Machine Retrieval Systems and Automated Procedures. Part A. Use of Automated Systems." *Journal of Medical Education* 40 # 1 (January, 1965): 46-49.
65	Feb.	"Is Youth Rejecting Science?" *Wilson Library Bulletin* 39 (February, 1965): 489, 509.
65	Mar.	"Daddy Warbucks and the School Librarian." *Wilson Library Bulletin* 39 (March, 1965): 573, 595.
65	Apr.	"A Better Class of Mouse." *Wilson Library Bulletin* 39 (April, 1965): 677. Also in *The Compleat Librarian,* 69-73. Cleveland: Press of Case Western Reserve University, 1971.
65	May.	"The Lifeblood of the Profession." *Wilson Library Bulletin* 39 (May, 1965): 785.
65	Jun.	"Of Wine, Waiters, and Librarians." *Wilson Library Bulletin* 39 (June, 1965): 903, 909. Also in *The Compleat Librarian,* 74 -76. Cleveland: Press of Case Western Reserve University, 1971.
65	Autumn.	Review of New *England Transplanted,* by Kenneth V. Lottich. In *Ohio History* 74 (Autumn, 1965): 275-76.
65	Fall.	Review of *The Papers of Thomas Jefferson,* vol 17, ed. Julian P. Boyd. In *Minnesota History* 45 (Fall, 1965): 295-96.
65	Sep.	"This Could be the Start." *Wilson Library Bulletin* 40 (September, 1965): 89.
65	Sep 1.	Review of *Parnassus on Main Street; a History of the Detroit Public Library,* by Frank B. Woodford. In *Library Journal* 90 # 15 (September I, 1965): 3424-25.
65	Oct.	"As You Wished You Were." *Wilson Library Bulletin* 40 (October, 1965): 179. Also in *The Compleat Librarian,* 77-80. Cleveland: Press of Case Western Reserve University, 1971.
65	Nov.	"A Renaissance in Library History?" *Wilson Library Bulletin* 40 (November, 1965): 281.

| 65 | Dec. | "Kinder, Kuche, und Bibliotheken." *Wilson Library Bulletin* 40 (December, 1965): 365. Also in *The Compleat Librarian, 81-83.* Cleveland: Press of Case Western Reserve University, 1971. |
| 65 | Dec. | "Librarians' Pugwash; or Index on the Cape." *Wilson Library Bulletin* 40 # 4 (December, 1965): 359 - 62. Also In "The *Documentation and the Organization of Knowledge,* ed. D. J. Foskett, 115 - 21. Hamden, Conn.: Archon Books, 1966. Abstracted in *Library Science Abstracts* 17 (1966): 298 - 9 # 66/797. |

1966

66.		***Documentation and the Organization of Knowledge*, ed. D. J. Foskett. Hamden, Conn.: Archon Books, 1966.**
66.		"The Present State of Education and Training in Documentation, Information Science, and Special Librarianship in the United States. " In *Proceedings of the 31st Hearing and Congress of the International Federation for Documentation in Cooperation with the American Documentation Institute, Washington, D. C., October 7-16, 1965,* 27-37. Washington, D. C.: Spartan Books, 1966.
66.		"The Challenging Role of the Reference Librarian." In *Reference, Research, and Regionalism,* 21 - 34. Selected papers from the 53rd Conference, Texas Library Association. Austin, Texas: The Association, 1966.
66.		"Foundations of a Theory of Reference Service. " In *Reference, Research, and Regionalism,* 13 - 20. Selected papers from the 53rd Conference, Texas Library Association. Austin, Texas: The Association, 1966. Also in *Knowing Books and Men: Knowing Computers, Too,* 196-206. Littleton, Colo.: Libraries Unlimited, 1973.
66	Jan.	"The Sheepskin Syndrome." *Wilson Library Bulletin* 40 (January, 1966): 461, 465.
66	Jan.	Review of *Science, Humanism, and Libraries,* by D. J. Foskett. In *Library Quarterly* 36 # 1 (January, 1966): 67-69.
66	Feb.	"Equus Donatus and the IRS." *Wilson Library Bulletin* 40) February, 1966): 545-52. Also in *The Compleat Librarian,* 84-86. Cleveland: Press of Case Western Reserve University, 1971.
66	Mar.	"What the Historian has been Missing." *Wilson Library Bulletin 40* (March, 1966): 639, 650. Also in *The Compleat Librarian, 87* - 90. Cleveland: Press of Case Western Reserve University, 1971.
66	Mar.	Review of *Focus on Information and Communication,* ed.

		Barbara Kyle. In *College and Research Libraries* 27 # 2 (March, 1966): 244-45.
66	Mar 15.	"Book Selection Wasteland." *Library Journal* 91 # 6 (March 15, 1966): 1332.
66	Apr.	"ALA Council." *Ohio Library Association Bulletin* 36 (April, 1966): 30.
66	Apr.	"Introduction" [to special issue on bibliographic organization]. *Wilson Library Bulletin* 40 # 8 (April, 1966): 703-5. Updates his and Margaret Egan's *Bibliographic Organization* . . . Chicago: University of Chicago, 1951.
66	Apr.	"NLW and the Cult of Reading." *Wilson Library Bulletin* 40 (April, 1966): 767. Also in *The Compleat Librarian*, 91 - 93. Cleveland: Press of Case Western Reserve University, 1971.
66	May.	"Of Comforts, Amenities, and Cats. " *Wilson Library Bulletin* 40 (May, 1966): 859. Also in *The Compleat Librarian*, 94- 96. Cleveland: Press of Case Western Reserve University, 1971.
66	Jun.	"Caveat Venditor. " *Wilson Library Bulletin* 40 (June, 1966): 955, 973. Also in *The Compleat Librarian*, 97-99. Cleveland: Press of Case Western Reserve University, 1971.
66	Summer.	"The Library: Institutional Deep-freeze or Intellectual Accelerator?" *Outlook* 3 # 4 (Summer, 1966): 6-9; published by Western Reserve University. Also in *The Library Binder* II, # 2 (December, 1966): 25-32.
66	Autumn.	Review of *New England Transplanted*, by Kenneth V. Lottich. In *Ohio History* 74 # 4 (Autumn, 1966): 275 - 76.
66	Sep.	"The Beginning of a Great Career." *SOLTAS News* 21 # 4 (September, 1966): 3-4; published by the Florida State University Library School.
66	Sep.	"The Librarian as Anthologist." *Wilson Library Bulletin* 41 (September, 1966): 89, 106. Also in *The Compleat Librarian*, 100-102. Cleveland: Press of Case Western Reserve University, 1971.
66	Sep 1.	Review of *Early Public Libraries; a History of Public Libraries in Great Britain Before 1850*, by Thomas Kelly. *Journal* 91 # 15 (September 1, 1966): 3912.
66	Oct.	"ALA Council at the New York Conference." *Ohio Library Association Bulletin* 36 (October, 1966): 28 - 29.
66	Oct.	"Je Crois qu'elle Ose Regarder mon Nez." *Wilson Library Bulletin* 41 (October, 1966): 215, 242.
66	Oct.	Review of *Classification Research*, Proceedings of the Second International Study Conference held at Hotel Prins

		Hamlet, Elsinore, Denmark, September 14-18, 1964, ed. Pauline Atherton. *In Library Quarterly* 36 # 4 (October, 1966), 356-58.
66	Oct 1.	Review of *Approaches* to *Library History,* Proceedings of the Second Library History Seminar, Florida State University Library School, March 4-6, 1965, Tallahassee, ed. John David Marshall. In *Library Journal* 91 # 17 (October 1, 1966), 4627.
66	Nov.	"The Golden Egg of Federal Support. " *Wilson Library Bulletin* 41 (November, 1966): 327, 348. Also in *The Compleat Librarian* 103 -105. Cleveland: Press of Case Western Reserve University 1971.
66	Dec.	"Cherchez 1 ' Homme. *Wilson Library Bulletin* 41 (December, 1966) 423, 435.
66	Dec.	"The Library: Institutional Deep- freeze or Intellectual Accelerator?" *The Library Binder* 14 # 2 (December, 19 66): 25-32. Also in *Outlook* 3 # 4 (Summer, 19 66): 3- 4.

<u>1967</u>

67.	**"Automated Information Exchange for Business and Industry. " In** *Report of* **a** *Rochester* **Area** *Conference on Technology Transfer and Innovation in Business and Industry,* **21 - 24. Rochester, N.Y.: University of Rochester and the State Technical Service: Administration, New York State Department of Commerce, 1967.**
67.	"Comments. " In *Proceedings of a Conference on Regional Medical Library Service,* eds. Barbara Denison, Robert G. Cheshier, and Alan M. Rees, 38- 52. Cleveland: Cleveland Medical Society Library and Western Reserve University, School of Library Science, 1967.
67.	"The Library Profession. " Introduction to *Peterson's Career and Adviser's Booklet to Librarianship and Information Science.* Princeton: Peterson's Guides, 1967.
67.	"Special Libraries; Why 'Special'?" In *Special Libraries: Problem: and Cooperative Potentials,* eds. Robert J. Havlik, Bill M. Woods, and Leona A. Vogt, 5 -1 6. Report Prepared for the President's National Advisory Commission on Libraries. Washington, D.C.: American Documentation Institute, 1967.
67.	"Beyond 1984: What's Past is Prologue. " ALA *Bulletin* 61 # 1 (January, 1967): 35-47. Abstracted in *Library Science Abstracts* 18 (1967): 103- 4 # 67/289. Replies by R. R. Shaw, *ALA Bulletin* 61 (March, 1967): 231-32; and R.

		H. McDonough, *ALA Bulletin* 61 (May, 1967): 457. Also in *Knowing Books and Men: Knowing Computers, Too*, 12-26. Littleton, Colo.: Libraries Unlimited, 1973.
67	Jan.	"The 'Trickseter' in Library Research." *Wilson Library Bulletin* 41 (January, 1967): 521, 533. Also in *The Compleat Librarian*, 106-8. Cleveland: Press of Case Western Reserve University, 1971.
67	Jan 1.	Review of *Who's Who in Library Service*, by Lee Ash, et al. In *Library Journal* 92 # 1 (January 1, 1967): 87.
67	Feb.	"Standard Lists; an Unstandardized View." *Wilson Library Bulletin* 41 (February, 1967): 615, 630. Also in *The Compleat Librarian*, 109-111. Cleveland: Press of Case Western Reserve University, 1971.
67	Mar.	"In Memoriam: Esther Piercy. " *Wilson Library Bulletin* 41 (March, 1967): 671.
67	Mar.	"You're Going on a Spree in 1973. " *Wilson Library Bulletin* 41 (March, 1967): 723, 738. Comment by H. G. Morehouse, *Wilson Library Bulletin* 41 (May, 1967): 887. Also in *The Compleat Librarian*, 112 -16. Cleveland: Press of Case Western Reserve University, 1971.
67	Mar 15.	Review of *Selected Readings in the History of Librarianship*, ed. John L. Thornton. In *Library Journal* 92 # 6 (March 15, 1967): 1132.
67	Apr.	"The Computer and the Chancellor." *Wilson Library Bulletin* 41 (April, 1967): 837, 856. Also in *The Compleat Librarian, 117*-19. Cleveland: Press of Case Western Reserve University 1971.
67	Apr.	"Report from the ALA Council. " *Ohio Library Association Bulletin* 37 (April, 1967): 28-29.
67	Apr.	Review of *ASLIB Conference* (1964). In *American Documentation* 18 # 2 (April, 1967): 115-16.
67	May.	"Librarians Against Machines." *Science* 156 # 3776 (May, 1967): 746-50. Revised in *Wilson Library Bulletin* 42 # 1 (September, 1967): 65-73. Abstracted in *Library Science Abstracts* 18 (1967): 211 # 67/575.
67	May.	"What's Wrong with Educational Excellence?" *Wilson Library Bulletin* 41 (May, 1967): 969, 985. Also in *The Compleat Librarian*, 120-23. Cleveland: Press of Case Western Reserve University, 1971.
67	Jun.	"An Aslib for America." *Wilson Library Bulletin* 41 (June, 1967): 1063-64.
67	Fall.	With Conrad H. Rawski. "The Diagram is the Message." *Library Resources and Technical Services* 11 # 4 (Fall, 1967): 487-98. Revised in *Journal of Typographic Research* 2 # 2 (April, 1968): 171-88.
67	Sep.	"Librarians Against Machines." *Wilson Library Bulletin* 42 #

		1 (September, 1967): 65-73. Revised from *Science* 156 # 3776 (May, 1967): 746-50.
67	Sep.	"The Phronemophobic ALA." *Wilson Library Bulletin* 42 (September 1967): 85, 104-105.
67	Sep.	"Robert S. Taylor." *College and Research Libraries* 28 (September 1967): 205-6.
67	Oct.	"More Library Schools?" *Ohio Library Association Bulletin* 37 (October, 1967): 5-9.
67	Oct.	"Report from the ALA Council." *Ohio Library Association Bulletin* 37 (October, 1967) : 28-29.
67	Oct.	"Try to Remember *Wilson Library Bulletin* 42 (October 1967): 215, 235. Also in *The Compleat Librarian*, 124-26. Cleveland: Press of Case Western Reserve University, 1971.
67	Oct 1.	"Bumbling Old ALA." *Library Journal* 92 (October 1, 1967): 3349-50.
67	Nov.	"Intellectual Freedom--Intellectual? Free?" *Wilson Library Bulletin* 42 (November, 1967): 323, 344. Comments by E. J. Gaines, L. C. Merritt, and H. L. Fletcher. *Wilson Library Bulletin* 42 (1968): 458-59, 565. Also in *The Compleat Librarian*, 127-30. Cleveland: Press of Case Western Reserve University, 1971.
67	Nov 1.	Review of *Move the Information; a Kind of Missionary Spirit*, Rowena W. Swanson. In *Library Journal* 92 # 19 (November 1967): 3975.
67	Dec.	"For a New Theory of the Leisure Class *Wilson Library Bulletin* 42 (December, 1967): 423, 436-37. Also in *The Compleat Librarian*, 131- 34. Cleveland: Press of Case Western Reserve University, 1971.

1968

68. **"An Epistemological Foundation for Library Science."** In *The Foundations of Access to Knowledge; a Symposium*, ed. Edward B. Montgomery, 7-25. Syracuse, N.Y.: Syracuse University Press, 1968.

68. "Federal Support for Income and Expenditures of Library Education Programs." In *North American Library Education: Directory and Statistics, 1966-1968*, ed. Frank L. Schick, 1-4. Chicago: American Library Association, 1968.

68. "Information Storage and Retrieval--Libraries." In *International Encyclopedia of the Social Sciences*, ed. David L. Sills, 7: 314-18. New York: Macmillan-Free Press, 1968.

68. "Libraries. " In *Living History of the World, 1968 Yearbook*, ed.

		George D. Stoddard, 318-19. New York: Stravon, 1968.
68	Jan.	"Playgirl of the Western World." *Wilson Library Bulletin* 42 (January, 1968): 529, 540.
68	Jan.	"What Librarianship is of Most Worth?" *Ohio Association of School Librarians Bulletin* 20 # 1 (January, 1968): 4 -9.
68	Feb.	"Is Documentation 'Camp'?" *Wilson Library Bulletin* 42 (February, 1968): 621, 634. Al so in *The Compleat Librarian, 135-38*. Cleveland: Press of Case Western Reserve University, 1971.
68	Mar-Apr.	"Of Librarianship, Documentation, and Information Science." *UNESCO Bulletin for Libraries* 22 # 2 (March -April, 1968): 58-65. Reprinted in *Key Papers in Information Science*, ed. Arthur W. Elias, 4 -11. Washington, D. C.: American Society for Information Science, 1971.
68	Mar.	"The People, Yes." *Wilson Library Bulletin* 42 (March, 1968): 727, 754. Also in *The Compleat Librarian*, 139-4l. Cleveland: Press of *Case* Western Reserve University, 1971.
68	Apr.	With Conrad H. Rawski. "The Diagram is the Message." *Journal of Typographic Research* 2 # 2 (April, 1968): *lll-88*. Revised from *Library Resources and Technical Services* 11 # 4 (Fall, 1967): 487 - 98. Also in *Knowing Books and Men: Knowing Computers, Too*, 27-40. Littleton, Colo.: Libraries Unlimited, 1973.
68	Apr.	"The Forty-first Chair." *Wilson Library Bulletin* 42 (April, 1968): 837, 862. Also in *The Compleat Librarian*, 142-44. Cleveland: Press of the Case Western Reserve University, 1971.
68	Apr.	"James V. Jones." *College and Research Libraries* 29 (April, 1968): 118-19.
68	Apr.	"Report from the ALA Council." *Ohio Library Association Bulletin* 38 (April, 1968): 36-37.
68	Apr.	Review of *Raking the Coals of History; the ALA Scrapbook of 1876*, by Edward G. Holley. In *Library Quarterly* 38 # 2 (April, 1968): 207-9.
68	May-Jun.	"On the Importance of Theory." *Rub-Off* 19 # 3 (May-June, 1968): 2-4.
68	May.	"An Ombudsman for ALA?" *Wilson Library Bulletin* 42 (May, 1968): 937, 950.
68	Jun.	"Of Parting, Umbrellas, and Prepositions," *Wilson Library Bulletin* 42 (June, 1968): 1037, 1054. Also in *The Compleat Librarian*, 145-47. Cleveland: Press of Case Wes tern Reserve University, 1971.
68	Jun 1.	"Dooley Dialect. Letters to the Editor." *Library- Journal* 93

		# 11 (June 1, 1968): 2185.
68	Jun 1.	Review of A *Chronology of Librarianship*, by Josephine Metcalf Smith. In *Library Journal* 93 # 11 (June I, 1968): 2219.
68	Sep.	"A Good Five-page Report. " *Wilson Library Bulletin* 43 (September, 1968): 71 -72. Also in *The Compleat Librarian, 148-50*. Cleveland: Press ~f Case Western Reserve University, 1971.
68	Oct.	"The Cerebral Foundations of Library Science." *Library School Review,* October, 1968, 3-6; published by Kansas State Teachers' College.
68	Oct.	"On the Importance of Theory." *Wilson Library Bulletin* 43 (October, 1968): 171, 174. Also in *The Compleat Librarian,* 151-53. Cleveland: Press of Case Western Reserve University, 1971.
68	Oct.	"Sing Me a Song of Social Significance; or, That's Not my Income--That's my Deficit: a Report from ALA Council." *Ohio Library Association Bulletin* 38 # 4 (October, 1968): 28-30.
68	Oct.	Review of *Manual of Public Libraries, Institutions and Societies in the United States and the British Provinces of North America*, by William J. Rhees. In *Library Journal* 93 # 17 (October, 1968): 3522.
68	Nov.	"Dichtung und Wahrheit." *Wilson Library Bulletin* 43 (November, 1968): 281-82. Also in *The Compleat Librarian,* 154-56. Cleveland: Press of Case Western Reserve University, 1971.
68	Dec.	"Isis and the Librarian's Quest for Unity. " *Wilson Library Bulletin* 43, (December, 1968): 373. Also in *Ohio Library Association* Bulletin 29 # 2 (April, 1959): 19, 21; and *The Compleat Librarian,* 157- 59. Cleveland: Press of Case Western University, 1971.

<u>1969</u>

69.	"**How Much is a Physicist's Inertia Worth?**" In *Reader in the Academic Library*, ed. Michael M. Reynolds, ed., 190-92. Washington, D. C.: NCR Microcard Editions, 1969. Reprinted from *Physics Today* 14 # 8 (August, 1961): 42-63.
69.	"Preface." In *Librarianship as a Profession in the Philippines; Proceedings of the First Regional Seminar of College and University Librarians, Bisayas and Mindanao Areas, November 11-13, 1968*, ed. Gorgonio D. Siega, iii-v. Dumaguete City, Philippine Islands: Silliman University Library, 1969.
69.	"'The Hungry Sheep Look Up;' Prolegomena to a Theory

		of Education for Librarianship." *Library School Review*, 1969, 3-7; published by Kansas State Teachers' College. Revised and expanded in *The Foundations of Education for Librarianship*, 493-502. New York: Wiley, Becker & Hayes, 1972.
69.		"Libraries. " In Living History of the World Yearbook, 1969, ed. George D. Stoddard, 314-15. New York: Stravon Educational Press and Parents' Magazine, 1969.
69.		With Anne S. McFarland. "Professional Aspects of Information Science and Technology." In Annual *Review of Information Science and Technology*, ed. Carlos A. Cuadra, 4: 439-71. Chicago: Encyclopaedia Britannica, 1969.
69.	Feb.	"Twelve Apostles and a Few Heretics [short version]." *News Letter* 68 (February, 1969): 24-26. Published by the Library Education Division of the American Library Association.
69.	Summer.	"Twelve Apostles and a Few Heretics [full version]." *Journal of Education for Librarianship* 10 # 1 (Summer, 1969): 3-10.
69	Sep 1.	"The Quiet Stir of Thought; or What the Computer Cannot do." *Library Journal* 94 # 15 (September I, 1969): 2875-80. First published with variant titles ("The Silent Stir of Though, and "The Quiet Stir of Thought") by the State University or New York (SUNY) as the Richardson Lecture for 1969 at the School of Library Science, Geneseo, N.Y. Also in *Library Association Record* 72 # 2 (February, 1970): 37 - 42; and *The Compleat Librarian*, 167-83. Cleveland: Press of Case Western Reserve University, 1971.
69	Sep 1.	Review of *World Guide* to *Libraries,* 2d ed., comp. Klaus G. Saur. In *Library Journal* 94 # 15 (September, 1969): 2893.
69	Oct 15.	Review of *A History of Library Education*, by Gerald Bramley. In *Library Journal* 94 # 18 (October 15, 1969): 3628.
69	Dec.	"The School of Library Science at Case Western Reserve University." *The Library Binder* 17 # 2 (December, 1969): 20-24.

<u>1970</u>

70.	***The Sociological Foundations of Librarianship*. Sarada Ranganathan Lectures, no. 3, 1967. New York: Asia Publishing House, 1970. Russian translation**

		by Viktor A. Polushkin, Moscow, 1973; Urdu translation, Lahore, 1980; Persian translation in *Journal of the Iranian Library Association* 10 # 1 (Spring, 1977): 1- 21.
70.		"The Library and Social Change." In *World Topics Yearbook,* 1970, 257-63. Lake Bluff, Ill.: United Educators, 1970.
70.		"Report on the Proposed Doctoral Program in the Department of Library Science, School of Graduate Studies, University of Toronto." 1970. 7p. Unpublished.
70.		"Research Needs Relating to the Aims and Needs of Graduate Library Education." In *A Study of the Research Needs of Library and Information Science Education; Final Report,* ed. Harold Borko, 21-46. Los Angeles: Institute of Library Research, University of California at Los Angeles, 1970.
70.	Winter.	Review of *The Case for Faculty Status of Academic Librarians,* ed. Lewis C. Branscomb. In *Educational Studies* 1 (Winter, 1970): 100.
70	Feb.	"The Quiet Stir of Thought; or What the Computer Cannot Do." *Library Association Record* 72 # 2 (February, 1970): 37 -42. Reprinted from *Library Journal* 94 # 15 (September I, 1969): 2875 -80. First published separately with variant titles ("The Silent Stir of Thought," and "The Quiet Stir of Thought") by the State University of New York (SUNY) at Geneseo, N. Y., 1969. Also in *The Compleat Librarian,* 167 - 83. Cleveland: Press of Case Western Reserve University, 1971.
70	Mar 15.	"Plus ça Change." *Library Journal* 95 # 6 (March 15, 1970): 979-86. Reprinted in *Library Lit. 1--the Best and Men: Knowing Computers, Too,* 57-64. Littleton, Colo.: Libraries Unlimited, 1973.
70	Apr.	"The Readiness is All." *Ohio Library Association Bulletin* 40 # 2 (April, 1970): 4-9. Also in *Knowing Books and Men: Knowing Computers, Too,* 57-64. Littleton, Colo.: Libraries Unlimited, 1973.
70	Apr.	"What is a Book that a Man May Know it?" *Bulletin of the Cleveland Medical Library* 17 # 2 (April, 1970): 32-43. Littleton, Colo.: Libraries Unlimited, 1973. Note also *Introduction to Library Science: Basic Elements of Library Service,* 67-73. Littleton, Colo.: Libraries Unlimited, 1976.
70	Apr 1.	Review of *Libraries and their Users,* by Paul Kaufman. In *Library Journal* 95 # 7 (April 1, 1970): 1299.

70	May-Jun.	"The Library School and its Dean." *Rub -Off* 21 # 3 (May - June, 1970): 30-33.
70	May 1.	Review of *Advances* in *Librarianship*, ed. Melvin J. Vogt. In *Library Journal* 95 # 9 (May 1, 1970): 1717.
70	Nov.	"President's Message. " *Beta Phi Mu Newsletter* 30 (November, 1970): 1-2.

1971

71.		*The Compleat Librarian.* Cleveland: Press of Case Western Reserve University, 1971. Selections from columns in the *Wilson Library Bulletin* entitled "Without Reserve."
71.		"Case Western Reserve University School of Library Science. " In *Encyclopedia of Library and Information Science*, eds. Allen Kent and Harold Lancour, 4:220 -28. New York: Marcel Dekker, 1971.
71.		"Causal Factors in Public Library Development." In *A Reader* in *American Library History*, e d. Michael H. Harris, 14 1 - 62. N.C.R. Microcard Editions. Washington, D. C.: National Cash Register *Co.*, 1971. Reprinted from *Foundations of the Public Library: the Origins of the Public Library Movement* in *New England, 1629-1855*, chapter 7. Chicago: University of Chicago Press, 1949.
71.		"The Expansion of the Social Library." In *A Reader* in *American Library History*, ed. Michael H. Harris, 45-53. N.C.R. Microcard Editions. Washington, D. C.: National Cash Register Co., 1971. Reprinted from *Foundations of the Public Library: the Origins of the Public Library Movement in New England, 1629-1855*, chapter 3. Chicago: University of Chicago Press, 1949.
71.		"Libraries." In *World Topics Yearbook, 1971*, 299-302. Lake Bluff, Ill.: United Educators, 1971.
71.		"On the Value of Library History." In *A Reader in American Library History*, ed. Michael H. Harris, 5-14. N.C.R. Microcard Editions. Washington, D. C.: National Cash Register Co., 1971. Also in *Landmarks of Library Literature, 1876-1976*, eds. Dianne J. Ellsworth and Norman D. Stevens, 153-71. Metuchen, N.J.: Scarecrow Press, 1976. Reprinted from *Library Quarterly* 22 # 3 (July, 1952): 240-51.
71	Mar-Apr.	"The Sociological Relationships of Information Science. " *Journal of the American Society for Information Science* 22 (March-April, 1971): 76-80.

71	Apr.	"President's Message." *Beta Phi Mu Newsletter* 31 (April, 1971): 1 - 3.
71	May 15.	Review of *Library History; an Examination Guidebook*, by James G. Olle. In *Library Journal* 96 (May 15, 1971): 1668.
71	Aug.	"Special Librarianship--How Special?" *Bulletin of the Texas Chapter, Special Libraries Association* 22 # 4 (August, 1972): 10-11.
71	Sep.	Review of *Classification and Information Control*, by the Classification Research Group. In *Journal of Documentation 27* (September, 1971): 220 - 22.
71	Sep.	Review of *Classification for a General Indexing Language*, by D. J. Foskett. In *Journal of Documentation* 27 (1971): 220-22.
71	Sep 1.	Review of *Library Humor; a Bibliothecal Miscellany*, ed. Norman D. Stevens. In *Library Journal* 96 (September 1, 1971): 2606.

1972

72.		***The Foundations of Education for Librarianship.* New York: Wiley, Becker & Hayes, 1972.**
72.		"For Whom do we Conserve? Or, What can You Do With a Gutenberg Bible?" Address to the Caxton Club (Chicago, 1972) reprinted in *Knowing Books and Men: Knowing Computers, Too*, 79-92. Littleton, Colo.: Libraries Unlimited, 1973.
72.		"Libraries." In *World Topics Yearbook*, 1972, 270 - 72. Lake Bluff, Ill.: United Educators, 1972.
72.		"Selected Bibliography." In *Research Memorandum on Internal Migration in the Depression*, by Warren S. Thompson, 69-82. Studies in the Social Aspects of the Depression. New York: Social Science Research Council, 1972. Reprint of 1937 ed.
72.	Winter.	Review of *Computers in Knowledge Based Fields*, by Charles A. Myers. In *Library Resources and Technical Services* 16 # 1 (Winter, 1972): 111-14.
72.	Jul-Aug.	"Two Decisive Decades; Documentation into Information Science." *American Libraries* 3 # 7 (July-August, 1972): 785-90. Reprinted in *Strategies for Change in Information Programs*, ed. William E. Hug, chapter 19. New York: R. R. Bowker, 1974.
72	Jul.	"Apologia pro Vita Nostra; the Librarian's Search for Identity." *Institute of Professional Librarians of Ontario Quarterly* 14 # 1 (July, 1972): 7 -19. Also in *Knowing Books and Men: Knowing Computers, Too*, 111-21.

		Littleton, Colo.: Libraries Unlimited, 1973.
72	Oct.	"The Self-destructing Diploma." *Ohio Library Association Bulletin* 42 (October, 1972): 4-8.
72	Oct 15.	Review of *Readings in Library History*, by Leslie W. Dunlap. In *Library Journal* 97 # 18 (October 15, 1972): 3295.

1973

73.		**Knowing Books and Men; Knowing Computers, Too. Littleton, Colo.: Libraries Unlimited, 1973. Collected essays.**
73.		"Aims and Content of Graduate Library Education." In *Targets for Research in Library Education,* ed. Harold Borko, 9-30. *Chicago:* American Library Association, 1973.
73.		"Libraries." In *World Topic Yearbook*, 1973, 305-6. Lake Bluff, Ill.: United Educators, 1973.
73.		"The Public Library in Perspective." In *The Metropolitan Library*, eds. Ralph W. Conant and Kathleen Molz, 101-23. Cambridge, Mass.: M.I.T. Press, 1973.
73.		"Toward a Theory of Librarianship and Information Science." *Ciencia da Informacao* 2 # 2 (1973): 87-98. Also *Knowing Books and Men: Knowing Computers, Too,* 92-110. Littleton, Colo.: Libraries Unlimited, 1973.

1974

74.		**"Libraries."** ***World Topics Yearbook***, **1974, 273-375. Lake Bluff, Ill.: United Educators, 1974.**
74.		With Margaret E. Anderson. "Souse Us in Literature." In *Access to the Literature of the Social Sciences and the Humanities*, ed. Morris Gelfand, 165-74. Flushing, N.Y.: Queens College Press, 1974. Includes "Implications of the Conference Papers for Library Education" followed by discussions, ibid., 165-86.
74	Jun.	"Mechanization, Librarianship, and the Bibliographic Enterprise. *Journal of Documentation* 30 # 2 (June, 1974): 153-69.
74	Jun 15.	Review of *Libraries and Librarianship in the West; a Brief History,* by Sidney L. Jackson. In *Library Journal* 99 # 12 (June 15, 1974): 1681.
74	Sep 15.	Review of *Advances in Librarianship,* ed. Melvin J. Voigt. In *Library Journal* 99 (September 15, 1974): 2044.

1975

75. With Margaret E. Anderson. *Education for Librarianship in the U.S. and Canada.* Occasional Paper no. 5. Liverpool, Canada: Liverpool Polytechnic, Department of Library and Information Science, 1975.

75. "The Administration of a Library School." In *Administrative Aspects of Education for Librarianship,* a *Symposium,* eds. Mary B. Cassata and Herman L. Totten, 294 -3 18. Metuchen, N.J.: *Scarecrow* Press, 1975.

75. With Margaret E. Egan. "Foundations of a Theory of Bibliography." In *Essays on Bibliography,* ed. Vito J. Brenni, 48-62. Metuchen, N. J.: Scarecrow Press, 1975. Reprinted from *Library Quarterly* 22 # 2 (April, 1952): 125- 37.

75. "Libraries. " In *World Topics Yearbook,* 1975, 278-79. Lake Bluff, Ill.: United Educators, 1975.

75. "What is Librarianship? " In *American Library Philosophy,* ed. Barbara McCrimmon, 165 - 71. Hamden, Conn.: Shoestring Press, 1975. Reprinted from *Louisiana Library Association Bulletin* 24 # 3 (Fall, 1961): 95-97.

75. Review of *The Association of American Library Schools,* 1915 -1 968; *an Analytical History,* by Donald G. Davis. In *American Reference Books Annual* 6 (1975): 129 -30 # 262.

75. Review of *Books and History,* by Robert B. Downs. In *American Reference Books Annual* 6 (1975): 63 # 136.

75. Review of *Librarianship; an Introduction to the Profession,* by Frank Atherton. In *American Reference Books Annual* 6 (1975): 62-63 # 135.

75. With Margaret E. Anderson. Review of *Libraries and Librarianship Around the World; a Brief History,* by Sidney L. Jackson. In *American Reference Books Annual* 6 (1975): 132-33 # 267.

75. Review of *Library Power; a New Philosophy of Librarianship,* by James Thompson. In *American Reference Books Annual* 6 (1975): 68-69 # 145.

75. Review of *Local History and the Library,* 2d ed., by John L. Hobbs. In *American Reference Books Annual* 6 (1975): 131 # 265.

75. Review of *The New Sabin; Books Described by Joseph Sabin and His Successors,* by Lawrence S. Thompson. In *American Reference Books Annual* 6 (1975): 3 # 5.

75. Review of *The Research Handbook; Guide to Reference Sources,* by Adrian A. Paradis. In *American Reference Books Annual* 6 (1975): 313- 14 # 695.

75. Review of *The* Story of *a Small Town Library; the Development of the Woodstock, N. Y., Library*, by Frances Rogers. In *American Reference Books Annual* 6 (1975): 135 # 270.

75. Review of *Thomas Bray's Grand Design; Libraries of the Church of England in America, 1694-1 785*, by Charles T. Laugh e r. In *American Reference Books Annual* 6 (1975): 133-34 # 268.

75 Jun. "The Physician and the Librarian; the Living Body and the Living Word." *Hartford Hospital Bulletin* 30 # 2 (June, 1975): 56-63. Abbreviated and reprinted in *Bulletin* of *the Cleveland Medical Library* 22 # 3 (July, 1976): 60 -64.

75 Oct. Review of *The Library of James Logan of Philadelphia, 1674-1751*, by Edward Woolf. In *Pennsylvania Magazine of History and Biography* 99 # 4 (October, 1975): 500 - 501.

75 Nov 15. Review of *World Trends in Library Education*, by Gerald Bramley. In *Library Journal* 100 # 20 (November 15, 1975): 2119.

1976

76. *Introduction* to *Library Science: Basic Elements* of *Library Service.* **Littleton, Colo.: Libraries Unlimited, 1976. Excerpted [in Chinese, tr. Chao-sheng Cheng]** in *Journal of Library & Information Science* **10 (April, 1984): 96 -110; 10 (October, 1984): 216-40; 11 (April, 1985): 86 -123; and 11 (October, 1985): 235-66.**

76. "Libraries: the Librarian of Congress." In *World Topics Yearbook*, 1976, 326-28. Lake Bluff, Ill.: United Educators, 1976.

76. "On the Value of Library History." In *Landmarks of Library Literature, 1876-1976*, eds. Dianne J. Ellsworth and Norman D. Stevens, 153- 71. Metuchen, N. J.: Scarecrow Press, 1976. And in *A Reader in American Library History*, ed. Michael H. Harris, 5-14. N.C.R. Microcard Editions. Washington, D. C.: National Cash Register Co., 1971. Reprinted from *Library Quarterly* 22 # 3 (July, 1952): 240-51.

76. Review of *Ainsworth Rand Spofford, Bookman and Librarian*, by John Y. Cole. In *American Reference Books Annual* 7 (1976): 133 # 208.

76. Review of *Bibliography of George Cumberland, 1754-1848 . . .* , by G. E. Bentley. In *American Reference Books Annual* 7 (1976): 613 # 1271.

76. Review of *British Library History; a Bibliography, 196.0-1972*, by Denis F. Keeling. In *American Reference Books Annual*

		7 (1976): 140 -42 # 225.
76.		Review of *Guide* to *Research in American Library History*, by Michael H. Harris. In *American Reference Books Annual* 7 (1976): 140 # 223.
76	Jan 1.	"Failure and Success; Assessing a Century." *Library Journal* 101 # 1 (January 1, 1976): 281-87.
76	Mar.	"Two Centuries of American Librarianship." *Bulletin of the American Society for Information Science* 2 # 8 (March, 1976): 39-40.
76	Sep 15.	Review of *Historical Introduction to Library Education; Problems and Progress*, by Carl M. White. In *Library Journal* 101 # 16 (September 15, 1976): 1838.77.

1977

77.		**"Foreword." In *A Community Elite and the Public Library*, by Pauline Wilson, xi -xiv. Westport, Conn. : Greenwood Press, 1977.**
77.		"Foreword." In *The Oral Antecedents of Greek Librarianship*, by H. Curtis Wright, ix-xii. Provo, Ut.: Brigham Young University Press, 1977. Also in 2d printing of this work (1978).
77.		"Foreword" and "Introduction." In *Ranganathan: a Pattern Maker. Syndetic Study of his Contribution*, by Anand P. Srivastava. New Delhi: Metropolitan Book Co., PVT Ltd., 1977.
77.		With Donald B. Cleveland. "The History and Foundations of Information Science." In *Annual Review of Information Science and Technology*, ed. Martha E. Williams, 12:249-75. White Plains, N. Y.: Knowledge Industry Publications for American Society of Information Science, 1977.
77.		"Libraries. " In *World Topics Yearbook*, 1977, 268-69. Lake Bluff, Ill.: United Educators, 1977.
77.		"Ranganathan; a Study." Foreword to *Ranganathan; a Pattern Maker*, by A. P. Srivastava, xiii-xvi. New Delhi: Metropolitan Books, 1977.
77.		Review of *Book Illustrators in 18th Century England*, by Hans Hammulmann and T. S. R. Boase. In *American Reference Books Annual* 8 (1977): 36-37 # 66.
77.		Review of *An Historical Introduction* to *Library Education; Problems and Progress* to *1951*, by Carl M. White. In *American Reference Books Annual* 8 (1977): 142 # 142.
77	Jan.	Review of *The Age of Jewett; Charles Coffin Jewett, 1846 - 1868*, by Michael H. Harris. In *Library Quarterly* 47 # 1

		(January, 1977): 58 - 61.
77	Jan.	Review of *Ainsworth Rand Spofford, Bookman and Librarian*, by John Y. Cole. In *Library Quarterly* 47 # 1 (January, 1977) : 58 - 61.
77	Winter.	Review of *Cannon's Bibliography* of *Library Economy*, 1876-1920, by Anne Harwell Jordan and Melborne Jordan. In *Journal of Library History* 12 # 1 (Winter, 1977): 79-80.

1978

78.	**With George S. Bobinski and Bohdan S. Wynar, eds. *Dictionary of American Library Biography*. Littleton, Colo.: Libraries Unlimited, 1978.**
78.	"Beals, Ralph Albert (1899-1954)." In *Dictionary of American Library Biography*, eds. George S. Bobinski, Jesse Hauk Shera, and Bohdan S. Wynar, 1 7 - 20. Littleton, Colo: Libraries Unlimited, 1978.
78.	"Ditzion, Sidney Herbert (1908 - 1975)." In *Dictionary of American Library Biography*, eds. George S. Bobinski, Jesse Hauk Shera, and Bohdan S. Wynar, 137-38. Littleton, Colo: Libraries Unlimited, 1978.
78.	"Egan, Margaret Elizabeth (1905 -1959)." In *Dictionary of American Library Biography*, eds. George S. Bobinski, Jesse Hauk Shera, and Bohdan S. Wynar, 158 - 59. Littleton, Colo: Libraries Unlimited, 1978.
78.	"Foreword. " In *Notable Books on Chinese Studies; a Selected, Annotated, and Subject Divided Bibliographic Guide*, by C. H. Lowe, v-vi. Taipei: China Printing Ltd., 1978.
78.	"Libraries. " In *World Topics Yearbook*, 1978, 289-91. Lake Bluff, Ill.: United Educators, 1978.
78.	"Report of the Chairman of the Publications Committee of the Rowfant Club, 1977." In *Rowfant Club Yearbook*, 1977, 50-52. Cleveland: The Rowfant Club, 1979.
78.	Response to Kenneth W. Thompson's "The Last Quarter-Century; Change, Challenge, and Catastrophe." In *Changing Times; Changing Libraries*, eds. George S. Bonn and Sylvia Faibisoff, 14-22. Proceedings of the Allerton Park Conference, 1976. Urbana, Ill.: University of Illinois, Graduate School of Library Science, 1978.
78.	"Taube, Mortimer (1910 -1 965)." In *Dictionary of American Library Biography*, eds. George S. Bobinski, Jesse Hauk Shera, and Bohdan S. Wynar, 512 -13. Littleton, Colo: Libraries Unlimited, 1978.
78.	Review of *ALA Yearbook; a Review of Library Events, 1978*.

78.		In *American Reference Books Annual* 9 (1978): 80 # 139.
Review of *Manual of Library Economy; a Conspectus of Professional Librarianship for Students and Practitioners*. In *American Reference Books Annual* 9 (1978): 72-73.
78.		Review of *The Printed Book in America*, by Joseph Blumenthal. In *American Reference Books Annual* 9 (1978): 20-21.
78	Jan.	Review of *The Nature of Knowledge; an Introduction for Librarians*, by D. A. Kemp. In *Library Quarterly* 48 # 1 (January, 1978): 93-94.
78	Spring.	"The Upside -down Library." *Utah Libraries* 21 # 1 (Spring, 1978): 11-19. Reprinted in *Library Lit. 9--the Best of 1978*, ed. Bill Katz, 115-27. Metuchen, N.J.: Scarecrow Press, 1979.
78	May 1.	Review of *The National Central Library; an Experiment* in *Library Cooperation*, by S. P. L. Filon. In *Library Journal* 103 # 9 (May 1, 1978): 946.
78	Summer.	"And Gladly Teach." *Journal of Education for Librarianship* 14 # 1 (Summer, 1978): 60-67.
78	Jul.	Review of *American Library History, 1876-1976*, ed. Howard W. Winger. In *Library Quarterly* 48 # 3 (July, 1978): 324-27.
78	Jul.	Review of *A Century of Service; Librarianship in the U. S. and Canada*, by Sidney L. Jackson and others. In *Library Journal* 48 # 3 (July, 1978): 324-27.
78	Aug 1.	Review of *Reform and Reaction; the Big City Public Library in American Life*, by Rosemary Ruhig DuMont. In *Library Journal* 103 # 14 (August 1, 1978): 1489.

<u>1979</u>

79.	**"Libraries: Libraries and Proposition 13." In *World Topics Yearbook, 1979*, 297- 99. Lake Bluff, I ll. : United Educators, 1979.**
79.	"Report of the Chairman of the Publications Committee of the Rowfant Club, 1978. " In *Rowfant Club Yearbook*, 1978, 50-52. Cleveland: The Rowfant Club, 1979.
79.	"The Upside -down Library." I n *Library Lit. 9 - -the Best of 1978*, ed. Bill Katz, 115 -27. Metuchen, N. J.: Scarecrow Press, 1979. Reprinted from *Utah Libraries* 21 (Spring, 1978): 11-19.
79.	Review of *The Generic Book; What it is and How it Works*, by Louis Shores. In *American Reference Books Annual* 10 (1979): 79 # 155.
79.	Review of A *History of the Principles of Librarianship*, by James Thompson. In *American Reference Books Annual* 10

		(1979): 80 # 156.
79.		Review of *Libraries and the Arts and Humanities*, by Charles G. Bolte. In *American Reference Books Annual* 10 (1979): 75 # 146.
79	Jan 15.	Review of *Milestones to the Present; Papers from Library History Seminar V*, ed. Harold Goldstein. In *Library Journal* 104 # 2 (January 15, 1979): 174.
79	Jul.	"Education for Librarianship; an Assessment and a Perspective." Review of *The Search for a Scientific Profession; Library Science Education in the U.S. and Canada*, by Lloyd Hauser and Alvin M. Schrader. In *Library Quarterly* 49 (July, 1979): 310 - 16.
79	Winter.	"The Spirit Giveth Life; Louis Round Wilson and Chicago's Graduate Library School." *Journal of Library History* 14 # 1 (Winter, 1979): 77 -83.

1980

80.	"Butler, Pierce." In ALA *World Encyclopedia of Library and Information Services*, ed. Robert Wedgeworth, 105- 6. Chicago: American Library Association, 1980. Also the 2d ed., 1986, 148 -49.
80.	"Hooded Candles: Wilmarth Sheldon Lewis." In *Rowfant Club Yearbook*, 1980, 66 -68. Cleveland: The Rowfant Club, 1980.
80.	"Librarianship, Philosophy of." In *ALA World Encyclopedia of Library and Information Services*, ed. Robert Wedgeworth, 314-17. Chicago: American Library Association, 1980. Also the 2d ed., 1986, 453 - 57.
80.	"Libraries." In *World Topics Yearbook*, 1980, 274- 77. Lake Bluff, Ill.: United Educators, 1980.
80.	Review of *As Much to Learn as to Teach; Essays in Honor of Lester Asheim*, eds. Joel Lee and Beth A. Hamilton. In *American Reference Books Annual* 11 # 146 (1980): 69.
80.	Review of *British Librarianship Today*, by W. L. Saunders. In *American Reference Books Annual* 11 # 254 (1980): 121.
80.	Review of *The Expected Role of Beginning Librarians; a Comparative Analysis from Administrators, Educators, and Young Professionals*, ed. R. Wilburn Clouse. In *American Reference Books Annual* 11 (1980): 122 # 256.
80.	Review of *History of the Public Library, Vigo County [Ind.], 1816 - 1975*, by Irene Roberts McDonough. In *American Reference Books Annual* 11 # 262 (1980): 125- 26.
80.	Review of *Librarians of Congress, 1802-1974*. In *American*

80.		*Reference Books Annual* 11 (1980): 69-70 # 147. Review of *Louis Shores, Author and Librarian; a Bibliography*, by John D. Marshall. In *American Reference Books Annual* 11 (1980): 70 # 148.
80	Jan.	"King of Miami; an Appreciation." *Ohio Library Association Bulletin* 50 # 1 (January, 1980): 14-18.

1981

81.		**"Across the Boundaries of Culture."** In *Library Education Across the Boundaries of Cultures; a Festschrift to Mark the Silber Jubilee Celebration of the Library Science Department,* ed. Anis Khurshid, 35-42. Karachi: Library Science Department, University of Karachi, 1981.
81.		"Libraries." In *World Topics Yearbook,* 1981, 289-91. Lake Bluff, Ill.: United Educators, 1981.
81.		"The Pathfinder's Burden." In *Metcalf, Downs, Kaser, and Shera at Eastern Illinois University, April 10, 1981.* Library Journal Special Report no. 21. New York: R. R. Bowker, 1981.
81.		Review of *Cambridge Encyclopedia of Archaeology,* ed. Andrew Sherratt. In *American Reference Books Annual* 12 (1981): 178-79.
81.		Review of *The Handicapped Librarian; a Study in Barriers,* by G. Garry Warren. In *American Reference Books Annual* 12 (1981): 145-46.
81.		Review of *Men of Achievement,* vol. 6. In *American Reference Books Annual* 12 (1981): 53.
81	Jan.	Review of *A Book for a Sixpence,* by David Kaiser. In *Library Quarterly* 51 # 1 (January, 1981): 104-7.

1982

82.	**"Casual Factors in Public Library Development."** In *Public Librarianship; a Reader,* ed. Jane Robbins-Carter, 12-41. Littleton, Colo: Libraries Unlimited, 1982). Reprinted from his *Foundations of the Public Library* ..., chapter 7. Chicago: University of Chicago, 1949.
82.	"Foreword." In *The Spirit of Inquiry; the Graduate Library School of Chicago, 1921-1951,* by John Richardson, xi-xiii. Chicago: American Library Association, 1982.
82.	"Libraries." In *World Topics Yearbook,* 1982, 314-17. Lake Bluff, Ill.: United Educators, 1982.

82	Winter.	"Louis Round Wilson (1876-1979): the Last of the Pioneers." In *Journal of Library History* 17 # 1 (Winter, 1982): 65-77.
82	Mar.	"Information Science and the Theory of Librarianship." In *International Information, Communication & Education* 1 # 1 (March, 1982): 9-16.
82	Jul.	"A Tribute." *Ohio Library Association Bulletin* 52 # 2 (July, 1982): 26-28. Excerpts from Shera's columns in *Ohio Library Association Bulletin*.

1983

| 83 | [Dec.] | **"Librarianship and Information Science." In the *Study of Information*, eds. Fritz Machlup and Una Mansfield, 379-88. New York: John Wiley & Sons, 1983. This work actually appeared in January, 1984.** |

1984

| 84 | Apr. | **Excerpt [in Chinese] from Shera's *Introduction to Library Science; Basic Elements of Library Service*, tr. Chao-sheng Cheng. *Journal of Library and Information Science* 10 (April, 1984): 96-110.** |
| 84 | Oct. | Excerpt [in Chinese] from Shera's *Introduction to Library Science; Basic Elements of Library Service*, tr. Chao-sheng Cheng. *Journal of Library and Information Science* 10 (October, 1984): 226-40. |

1985

| 85 | Apr. | **Excerpt [in Chinese] from Shera's *Introduction to Library Science; Basic Elements of Library Service*, tr. Chao-sheng Cheng. *Journal of Library and Information Science* 11 (April, 1985): 86-123.** |
| 85 | Oct. | Excerpt [in Chinese] from Shera's *Introduction to Library Science; Basic Elements of Library Service*, tr. Chao-sheng Cheng. *Journal of Library and Information Science* 11 (October, 1985): 235-66. |

1986

86. "**Butler, Pierce.**" In *ALA World Encyclopedia of Library and Information Services*, **148-49. 2d ed. Chicago: American Library Association, 1986. Revised from the 1st ed., 1980, 105-6.**

86. "Librarianship, Philosophy of." In *ALA World Encyclopedia of Library and Information Services*, 453-57. 2d ed. Chicago: American Library Association, 1986. Revised from 1st ed., 1980, 314-17.

INDEX

A

"Accent on Youth: the Significance of A.L.A. Reorganization for the Young Librarian" 66
Access to the Literature of the Social Sciences and the Humanities 101
"Across the Boundaries of Culture" 108
action theory 58
"The Administration of a Library School" 102
"Administration of the Library – Technical Operations" 69
Administrative Aspects of Education for Librarianship, a Symposium 102
"Advances in Documentation and Library Science, vol.2" 76
"The Age Factor in Employment: a Classified Bibliography" 64
"The Age of Paradox" 89
"Aims and Content of Graduate Library Education" 101
"ALA Council" 91
"ALA Council at the New York Conference" 91
"To the Alumni: Message of the Dean" 72
American Documentation 19, 68, 70, 71, 73-79, 90, 93
　editor *see* Tate, Vernon D.;
American Documentation Institute – ADI 19, 20, 24, 26, 30, 40, 92
　see also National Microfilm Association
　president *see*　Tate, Vernon D.; Taube, Mortimer; Evans, Luther
American Educators Encyclopedia 86
American Libraries 100
American Library 78
American Library Association – ALA 21, 25, 72, 73, 74, 81, 83, 86, 94, 97, 101, 107, 108
　ALA Bulletin 65, 66, 71, 73, 75, 79, 84, 87, 92, 93

ALA World Encyclopedia of Library and Information Services 107, 110
　Division of Cataloging and Classification 68, 70
　Library Education Division 97
American Library Philosophy 81, 102
American Notes and Queries 85
American Reference Books Annual 102-104, 106-108
American Scientist 75
American Society for Information Science (ASIS) 1, 40, 47, 95
　fragmentation 46
American Society for Metals
　grant for Western Reserve Documentation Center 28
American Society of Mechanical Engineers 81
Americana Corporation　81
Anderson, Margaret E. 101, 102
Annual Review of Information Science and Technology 97, 104
Anthoensen Press 71
"Apologia pro Vita Nostra; the Librarian's Search for Identity" 100
apprentice system 5
Archon Books 78-84, 86, 88, 90
"Areas for Research" 74
"As You Wished You Were" 89
Ash, Lee 93
Asia Publishing House 88, 97
ASLIB 76,
"An Aslib for America" 93
ASME Design Engineering Conference 81
Association of American Library Schools Bulletin　77
Association of College and Research Libraries – ACRL Monographs 74
Atherton, Frank 102
Austin, TX 90
"Automated Information Exchange for Business and Industry" 92
"Automation and the Reference Librarian" 87

"Automation Without Fear" 79, 80

B

"Background Courses in Education for Librarianship" 77
"Backward to Normalcy" 87
"The Bad-Humor Man" 82
"Bamboo and Silk and the Art of Talking Back" 85
"Barred Gates: a Librarian's Plea for Freedom" 66
Battelle Memorial Institute *see* Columbus, Ohio
Beacon, Betty 78
Beals, Ralph 22, 24
"Beals, Ralph Albert (1899-1954)" 105
Beetle, Clare 70
"The Beginning of a Great Career" 91
"The Beginnings of Systematic Bibliography in America, 1642-1799" 70, 71
"In the Beginning there was the Word" 75
Bentley, G. E. 103
Berry, Madeline M. 75
Beta Phi Mu Newsletter 99, 100
"A Better Class of Mouse" 89
"Beyond 1984: What's Past is Prologue" 92
"Bibliographic Management" 71
Bibliographic Organization 70, 71, 91
"Bibliotecas del Mañana" 84
Bibliotecología y Documentacion; Estudios y Trabajos [Serie A] 86
"Bibliotheque de la Demain" 84
"Die Bibliothek von Morgen" 84
Bickham, Helen (*see* Shera, Helen Bickham)
Billings, John Shaw 13
"Biographical Notes: L.S. Dutton; E.W. King" 76
"Biographical Sketch: Russel S. Dozer" 76
Blumenthal, Joseph 106
BMI *see* Columbus, Ohio; Battelle Memorial Institute
Boase, T. S. R. 104
Bobinski, George S. 105
Bolte, Charles G. 107
"The Book Catalog and the Scholar; a RE-examination of an Old Partnership" 82, 83
Book Catalogs 82, 83
"A Book for Burning" 84
"Book Selection Wasteland" 91
Borko, Harold 98, 101
Bowers, David Fredson 68, 70
Bowker, R. R. 100, 108
Boyd, Julian P. 70, 71, 73, 74, 76, 78, 89
Bradford, S. C. 69, 72, 86
Bramley, Gerald 103
Branscomb, Lewis C. 98
Brenni, Vito J. 72, 102
Briet, Suzanne 71
Brigham Young University Press 104
Brough, Kenneth J. 73
Brown, Herbert Ross 67
Buhler, Curt F. 70
Bulletin of Bibliography 64
Bulletin of the American Society for Information 104
Bulletin of the Cleveland Medical Library 98, 103
Bulletin of the Ohio Library Association 79
"Bumbling Old ALA" 94
Bush, Vannevar 17
Butler, Pierce 22
"Butler, Pierce" 107, 110
Butterfield, Herbert 76

C

"Call to Action" 65
Cambridge, Massachusetts 20
card catalogs 14
"Cards is Cards" 82
Carnegie Corporation 18, 19, 26
Case Western Reserve University 1, 2, 6, 22, 23, 29, 34, 36, 37, 42, 45, 62, 88, 91
  Archives 2
  Documentation Center *see* Center for Documentation and Communication
  library school at ~ 21, 26, 28, 30-33, 37, 39, 92

INDEX

News Bulletin 72
president of ~ *see* Millis, John Schoff
~ Press *see* Press of Case Western Reserve University
"Case Western Reserve University School of Library Science"
Cassata, Mary B. 102
"Causal Factors in Public Library Development" 68, 99, 108
"Caveat Venditor" 91
Caxton Club 100
"The Center of Documentation – a Regional Approach" 68
Center for Documentation and Communication Research – CDCR 26, 27, 28, 30-33, 35-37, 39, 77, 88
Centro de Documentación e Información de Asuntos Municipales Doctor Alcides Greca 86
"The Cerebral Foundations of Library Science" 96
"The Challenging Role of the Reference Librarian" 90
Champaign, Illinois 77, 78
"Changing Concepts of Classification; Philosophical and Educational Implications" 88
"The Changing Philosophy of Bibliographic Classification" 79
Changing Times; Changing Libraries 105
Cheng, Chao-sheng 109
Cherry, Colin 49
Cheshier, Robert G. 92
Chicago 69-74, 81, 83, 91, 94, 97, 99, 100, 101, 107, 108, 110
  Graduate Library School – GLS 2, 8, 14, 22, 23, 24, 28, 30, 31, 59
  University of 2, 15, 18, 20, 29 70, 71, 91
  ~ Press 69, 71 13, 17, 69, 71, 99
  Director of Libraries *see* Beals, Ralph
"Chicago Conference on Bibliographic Organization" 71
The Clarification, Unification, and Integration of Information Storage and Retrieval 80

"Classification as the Basis of Bibliographic Organization" 71
"Classification at Dorking; the International Study Conference on Classification for Information Retrieval" 77
"Classification; Current Functions and Applications to the Subject Analysis of Library Materials" 72
Classification Research Group 100
The Classified Catalog; Basic Principles and Practices 74
Clemons, Harry 74
Cleveland, Donald B. 104
Cleveland, Ohio 2, 21, 22, 24, 26, 27, 72, 77, 80-82, 84-99, 106, 107
Cleveland Medical Society Library 92
"Cloudland Revisited" 80
Clouse, R. Wilburn 107
Cole, John Y. 103, 105
College and Research Libraries 68, 69, 70, 71, 73, 76, 80, 81, 85, 91, 94, 95
"College and University Libraries" 81
"College Librarianship and Educational Reform" 66
"The College Library of the Future" 65
Columbia University, New York 2, 6, 7,
  School of Library Service 72
Columbus, Ohio 27
  Battelle Memorial Institute – BMI 26
  president *see* Williams, Clyde
"Of Comforts, Amenities, and Cats" 91
Commager, Henry Steele 67
"Common Languages in ibrarianship and Documentation" 79
"Communicating Office of Education Statistics" 78
Communication of Specialized Information; Papers Presented Before the Seventeenth Annual Conference of the Graduate School of the University of Chicago, August 11-15, 1954 73
A Community Elite and the Public Library 104
The Compleat Librarian 80-99
computer(s) 1, 15, 17, 18, 31, 46, 56, 60

general-purpose ~ GE 225 28
"The Computer and the Chancellor" 93
"Cooperative Book Club" 66
El Correo 84
"Council Votes to Probe Civil Rights Cases" 66
counting machines
  see tabulating machines
Le Courrier 84
Covington, Mary 80
Crosby, Lockwood & Son 72
"Cult of the Audio-visual" 81
"A Curriculum for Mr. Ciardi" 81
Curti, Merle 68, 79
Cutter, Charles A. 43

D

"Daedalus, Icarus, and the Technological Revolution" 88
"Daddy Warbucks and the School Librarian" 89
Danger Spots in World Population 64
Danton, Emily V. 66
data
  mechanized retrieval
"Darwin, Bacon, and Research in Librarianship" 87
Davis, Donald G. 102
Davis, Watson 16
Decisiones Gerenciales y Computadoras 84
"In Defense of Diversity" 86
"In Defense of Miss Groby" 84
Denison, Barbara 74, 75, 81, 86, 92
Department of Health, Education, and Welfare *see* U.S. Department of Health, Education, and Welfare
Dewey, Melville 25
"Developments in Machine Literature Searching" 80
"The Diagram is the Message" 93, 95
"Dichtung und Wahrheit" 96
Dictionary of American Library Biography 105
"The Dignity and Advancement of Bacon" 81
"Dimensions of the Master's Program" 87

"Discipline, Dissent, and Documentation" 83
"The 'Dismal Science' and Librarianship" 81
District of Columbia Libraries 75
"Ditzion, Sidney Herbert (1908-1954)" 105
Documentation 72
Documentation and Information Retrieval 76
Documentation and the Organization of Knowledge 79-83, 87, 90
Documentation Center *see* Center for Documentation and Communication Research – CDCR
Documentation in Action 75
"Documentation in Action" 75
"Documentation in the United States" 70
"Documentation; its Scope and Limitations" 71
Documentation on a Regional Basis 68
"D.R.S. To the G.I.S." 84
"Dooley Dialect. Letters to the Editor" 95
Downs, Robert B. 102
Dulap, Leslie W. 101
DuMont, Rosemary Ruhig 106

E

Eastman Kodak 16, 40
Eaton, Thelma 77, 78
"An Eddy in the Western Flow of American Culture; the History of Printing and Publishing in Oxford, Ohio, 1872-1841" 65
"Editorial" 73, 76
"Editorial: Antidote for Tranquilizers" 78
"Editorial: Fundamental Research; a Few Fundamentals" 75
"Editorial: The Historian and Documentation" 78
"Editorial: A House Divided" 74
"Editorial: Librarians and the Sputnik" 77
"Editorial: Loue par Ceux-ci..." 76
"Editorial: A Mandate for Documentation" 79

INDEX

"Editorial: Of Mountains, and Coffee, and Documentation" 77
"Editorial: Needed--'Creative Documentation'" 75
"Editorial: A New High at Lehigh" 79
"Editorial: The New World's Debt to the Old" 77
"Editorial: The Parlement of Foules" 77
"Editorial: Ralph Albert Beals and Jack Cassius Morris" 74
"Editorial: The Renaissance of Classification" 78
"Editorial: A Science Full of Living Problems" 78
"Editorial: The Solitary Esophagus" 78
"Editorial: Thoughts on New Year's Eve" 76
"Editorial: Toward the Formation of a Library Editors' Council" 74
"Editorial: The Truth, the Whole Truth..." 74
"Editorial: UNESCO – Ten Years After" 76
"Education for Documentation" 77
"Education for Librarianship; an Assessment and a Perspective" 107
"Education for Librarianship; an Integrated Approach" 73
*Education for Librarianship in the U.S. and Canada*102
The Education of Science Information Personnel 88
"An Educational Program for Special Librarians" 80
Educational Studies 98
"Effect of Machine Methods on the Organization of Knowledge" 72
Egan, Margaret E. 17, 18, 22, 23, 27, 69, 70-74, 77, 86, 91, 102
  death 31
"Egan, Margaret Elizabeth (1905-1959)" 105
Ekirch, Arthur A. 68
Ellsworth, Diane J. 99, 103
"Emergence of a New Institutional Structure for the Dissemination of Specialized Information" 73

"On the Encouragement of Reading" 88
Encyclopedia Americana 81
Encyclopedia Britannica 97
Encyclopedia International 86
Encyclopedia of Library and Information Science 99
Enquiry Concerning the Professional Education of Librarians and Documentalists: Report to the Joint Committee of the International Federation of Library Associations and of the International Federation for Documentation 71
"An Epistemological Foundation for Library Science" 94
"The Epistle of Paul to the Pedants" 86
"Equus Donatus and the IRS" 90
Essays Honoring Lawrence C. Wroth 71
Essays on Bibliography 72, 102
Europe 39
Evans, Charles 85
Evans, Luther 19, 20
"An Exchange of Correspondence" 66
Examen del Estado Actual de la Biblioteconomía y de la Documentación 86
"The Expansion of the Social Library" 99

F

"Failure and Success; Assessing a Century" 104
"Far Above Cayugas Waters" 85
"Federal Support for Income and Expenditures of Library Education Programs" 94
"A Few Coals to Newcastle" 66
Fifteeth Annual Conference of the GLS 18
Filon, S. P. L. 106
Fletcher, H. L. 94
Flexner, Abraham 41
Florida State University Library School 91
"Formulate a Professional Philosophy" 84
"The Forty-first Chair" 95

Foskett, D. J. 78-84, 86, 88, 90, 100
The Foundations of Access to Knowledge; a Symposium 94
The Foundations of Education for Librarianship 97, 100
"Foundations of a Theory of Bibliography" 72, 102
"Foundations of a Theory of Reference Service" 90
Foundations of the Public Library: the Origins of the Public Library Movement in New England, 1629-1855 69, 99, 108
Frarey, Carlyle J. 80
"Fremont Rides Through the Dewey Fog" 82
"From the President" 86-88
Fussler, Herman H. 5
The Future of the Medical School Library 87
"The Future, Too, is Prologue" 88

G

Gains, E. J. 94
Galsworthy, John
    Forsyte novels 2
Gelfand, Morris 101
General Electrical – GE 28, 40
giant brain 18
"And Gladly Teach" 106
GLS at Chicago *see* Chicago, Graduate Library School
"The Golden Egg of Federal Support" 92
"A Good Five-page Report" 96
Goodspeed, Edgar J. 65
Goff, Frederick R. 71
Goldstein, Harold 107
Goldwyn, A. J. 88
Grant, Thirza 21
The Great Depression 4, 7,
Grolier Incorporated 86
"The 'Guide' Stands First" 85
Guidebook 100
Guss, Carolyn 78

H

Hamden, CT 78-84, 86, 88, 90
Hamilton, Beth A. 107
Hammulmann, Hans 104

"Handmaidens of the Learned World" 64
Harris, Michael H. 99, 103, 104
Hartford Hospital Bulletin 103
Hauser, Lloyd 107
Havlik, Robert J. 92
Hawken, William M. 85
Hawthorne, Nathaniel 85
Heckert, Winfield 1
Hessel, Alfred 71
Helmuth, Ruth 2
Herald of Library Science 83-85
high school 13
Hines, Theodore C. 89
Historians, Books, and Libraries 72
History 73
"The History and Foundations of Information Science" 104
Hobbs, John L. 102
Hockett, Homer C. 68
Hollerith, Herman 13
    Hollerith machines 13, 16
Holley, Edward G. 85, 95
"Hooded Candles: Wilmarth Sheldon Lewis" 107
hospital 10
"How Engineers Can Keep Abreast of Professional and Technical Literature" 81
"How Much is a Physicist's Inertia Worth?" 80, 96
Hug, William E. 100
Hughes, Raymond M. 4, 6
Humphry, Hurbert H., Senator 30
"'The Hungry Sheep Look up;' Prolegomena to a Theory of Education for Librarianship" 96, 97
Hunt, Morton 57
H. W. Wilson Company 28

I

idea service 43
Illini Union Bookstore 77, 78
"On the Importance of Theory" 95, 96
Indian Librarian 84, 85
"Influences on American Culture" 68

INDEX

information
  explosion 29, 53
  movement 18
  problem (crisis) 19, 20, 26, 27, 29, 33, 34, 35, 37, 52
  retrieval 36, 37, 40, 43
  systems of ~ access 6, 26, 52
  theory 47-50, 52
Information Resources; a Challenge to American Science and Industry 77
Information Retrieval and Machine Translation 79
Information Retrieval Today: Papers Presented at the Institute Conducted by the Library School and the Center for Continuation Study, University of Minnesota, September 19-22, 1962 83
Information Systems in Documentation 76
Institute of Professional Librarians of Ontario Quarterly 100
"The Instrumentality of Data" 42
International Encyclopedia of the Social Sciences Living History of the World, 1968 Yearbook 94
Interscience Publishers 75, 76, 79
Illinois Library Association
  ILA Record 72
Indiana University 78
"Information Science and the Theory of Librarianship" 108
"Information Storage and Retrieval – Libraries" 94
Institute of Library Research 98
"Intellectual Freedom – Intellectual? Free?" 94
International Information, Communication & Education 109
Introduction to Sociology 2
"Introduction" to *Documentation* 86
Introduction to Library Science: Basic Elements of Library Service 98
Introduction to Library Science; Basic Elements of Library Service [in Chinese] 109
Introduction to *Peterson's Career and Adviser's Booklet to Librarianship and Information Science* 92
"Introduction and Welcome" 88

Iowa State University
  President of ~ (see also Hughes, Raymond M.) 4
"Is Documentation 'Camp'?" 95
"Isis and the Librarian's Quest for Unity" 79, 96

J

Jackson, Sidney I. 101, 102, 106
James, William 57, 58
"James V. Jones" 95
"Je Crois qu'elle Ose Regarder mon Nez" 91
Jordan, Anne Harwell 105
Jordan, Melborne 105
Journal of Cataloging and Classification 69, 74, 75
Journal of the American Society for Information Science 99
Journal of Documentation 88, 100, 101
Journal of Education for Librarianship 80, 86, 97, 106
Journal of the Iranian Library Association 98
Journal of Library & Information Science 109
  World Topics Yearbook 103
Journal of Library History 105, 107, 109
Journal of Medical Education 89
Journal of Typographic Research 93, 95

K

Kaiser, David 108
Kansas State Teachers' College 96, 97
Katz, Bill 106
Kaufman, Paul 81
Kaula, P. N. 88
"On Keeping Up with Keeping Up" 82
Keeling, Dennis F. 103
Kelly, Thomas 91
Kemp, D. A. 106
Kent, Allen 26, 27, 30, 31, 32, 36, 37, 74-77, 79, 99
Keppel, Frederick J. 16, 17
Key Papers in Information Science 95
Khurshid, Anis 108
"Kinder, Kuche, und Bibliotheken" 90

King, Edgar "Ned" Weld 2 – 8
  Miami's first professionally trained librarian 4
"King of Miami; an Appreciation" 108
Kingery, Robert E. 82, 83
Knopf, Alfred A. 64
Knowing Books and Men; Knowing Computers, Too 90, 93, 95, 98, 100, 101
"Knowledge Goes Berserk" 76
Kruzas, Anthony T. 85
Kurier 84
Kyle, Barbara 91

L

Lahore 98
Lake Bluff, IL 86, 98, 99, 101-108
Lancour, Harold 99
Landmarks of Library Literature, 1876-1976 99, 103
"The Last Quarter-Century; Change, Challenge, and Catastrophe" 105
Laugh, Charles T. 103
Lawler, John 71
Lee, Joel 107
"The Librarian and the Machine" 80
"The Librarian as Anthologist" 91
"Librarians Against Machines" 93
"The Librarian's 'Changing World'" 64
"The Librarians' New Frontier" 75
"Librarians' Pugwash; or Index on the Cape" 90
"Of Librarians and Other Aborigines" 87
"Librarianship and Information Science" 109
"Librarianship as a Career" 86
Librarianship as a Profession in the Philippines; Proceedings of the First Regional Seminar of College and University Librarians, Bisayas and Mindanao Areas, November 11-13, 1968 96
"Of Librarianship, Documentation, and Information Science" 95
"Librarianship in a High Key" 75
"Librarianship, Philosophy of" 107, 110

"Libraries" 94, 97, 99, 101, 102, 105, 107, 108
Libraries 64
Libraries and the Organization of Knowledge 78-84, 86-88
"Libraries and Museums" 67
"*Libraries are for Growing*" 84
"Libraries, History of" 86
"Libraries: Libraries and Proposition 13" 106
Libraries Unlimited 90, 93, 95, 98, 100, 101, 105
"The Library of the Future; a WLB Symposium" 88
"The Library and Social Change" 98
The Library Binder 91, 92, 97
Library Education Across the Boundaries of Cultures; a Festschrift to mark the Silver Jubilee Celebration of the Library Science Department 108
"The Library: Institutional Deep-freeze or Intellectual Accelerator?" 91, 92
Library Instructional Integration on the College Level 74
Library Journal 64, 65, 76, 77-80, 83-85, 87, 89, 91-101, 103-107
  Library Journal Special Report no.21 108
Library Literature 106
Library of Congress 19, 69
  Descriptive Cataloging Division 70
"The Library of the Future" 84, 85
The Library of Tomorrow 17
"The Library Profession" 92
Library Resources and Technical Services 77, 80, 82, 83, 93, 95
"The Library School and its Dean" 99
Library School Review 96, 97
Library Science Abstracts 79, 80, 83, 88, 90, 92, 93
Library Science Today: Ranganathan Festschrift 88
Library Trends 72, 76, 87, 88
Library Quarterly 65, 67-73, 81, 82, 85, 88, 90, 95, 99, 102, 103-108
"The Lifeblood of the Profession" 89

INDEX 119

"The Literature of American Library History" 68
"Little Girls Don't Play Librarian" 83
Littleton, Colorado 90, 93, 95, 98, 100, 101, 105
Liverpool Polytechnic Department of Library and Information Science 102
Living History of the World Yearbook, 1969 97
Los Angeles, California 98
Lottich, Kenneth V. 89, 91
"Louis Round Wilson (1876-1979): the Last of the Pioneers" 109
Louisiana Library Association Bulletin 81, 102
Lovejoy, Arthur O. 76
Lowe, C. H. 105

M

Machine Literature Searching "Foreword" 75
"Machine Retrieval Systems and Automated Procedures. Part A. Use of Automated Systems" 89
Machlup, Fritz 109
Macmillan [publishers] 67
Free Press 94
magnetic tape 25
Manley, Marian C. 67
Mansfield, Una 109
Manual for Use in the Cataloging of Audio-visual Materials for a High School Library, "Preface" 74
Manual of Document Reproduction and Selection Review of Documentation 76
Marshall, John David 92, 108
Massachusetts Institute of Technology – MIT 26
conference on application of machines to scientific informatiton 18
McCrimmon, Barbara 81
McDermott, John Francis 82
McDonough, Irene Roberts 107
McDonough, R. H. 93
McFarland, Anne S. 97
McGraw-Hill 64, 65
McManaway, James G. 70

Mead, George Herbert 54
"Mechanization, Librarianship, and the Bibliographic Enterprise" 101
mechanized information handling 14, 17
literature search 21, 25, 32
see also Davis, Watson
mechanized information retrieval 26, 28, 34, 35
access to databanks 41
Memex 17
"In Memoriam: Esther Piercy" 93
"In Memoriam: Margaret E. Egan" 78
"Member No. 3!" 65
Merritt, L. C. 94
Metropolitan Book Co. 104
Miami University, Ohio 3, 4, 6, 8, 9
Library 5, 9, 10
President of ~, (*see also* Hughes, Raymond M.) 4
Microfilm 16, 24
decline of ~ 19
microphotography 16, 17, 19, 24, 39
Miller, Perry 67
Millis, John "Jack" Schoff 10, 21, 22, 23, 24, 27, 32
Minicard system 16, 25
Minneapolis, Minnesota 83
Minnesota History 70, 71, 74, 76, 78, 89
"Mirror for Documentalists" 75
Mississippi Valley Historical Review 67, 68, 72, 74, 75, 77
Monaghan, Jay 70
Montgomery, Edward B. 94
"More Library Schools?" 94
Morehouse, H. H. 93
Morgan, Charles 68
Morison, Samuel Eliot 67
Moscow 98
"My Year in Library School; Some Second Thoughts" 78
Myers, Charles A. 100

N

National Advisory Commission on Libraries 92
National Archives 67
National Cash Register Co. 99

National Library of Medicine 81
National Institutes of Health 28
National Microfilm Association 19
   see also American Documentation Institute - ADI
National Science Foundation 28, 36, 85
New Delhi 104
"For a New Theory of the Leisure Class" 94
"New Tools for Easing the Burden of Historical Research" 78
New York 72, 74, 75, 79-83, 86, 88, 94, 95, 97-100
News Letter of the American Association of Library Schools 75
News Letter 97
"NLW and the Cult of Reading" 91
North American Library Education: Directory and Statistics, 1966-1968 94
"Not Novel but Bears Repeating" 78
Notable Books on Chinese Studies; a Selected, Annotated, and Subject Divided Bibliographic Guide 105

O

"O! Medium, O! Media" 85
"Objectives of the School of Library Science" 80
Office of Strategic Services – OSS 13, 15
Ohio Association of School Librarians Bulletin 95
Ohio Historical Quarterly 79
Ohio History 82, 89, 91
Ohio Library Association Bulletin 79, 86-88, 91, 93-97, 101, 108
"Ohio Library Association. Notes on State Library Association Activities, 1963-1964" 86
Ohio State Archaeological and Historical Quarterly 65, 70
Ohioana; of Ohio and Ohioans 86
Olle, James G. 100
"An Ombudsman for ALA?" 95
"On the Value of Library History" 103
The Oral Antecedents of Greek Librarianship 104

OSS   *see* Office of Strategic Services
Outlook 91, 92
Oxford, Ohio 3, 4, 7, 13
  (*see also* Miami University)

P

Pakistan Library Review 83, 84
Palmer, Bernard I. 72, 79, 81, 85
Papers of the Conference Within a Conference, July 16-18, 1963 86
Paradis, Adrian A. 102
Parker, Ralph 16
Parker, Wyman 88
Parsons, Edward A. 72
"Of Parting, Umbrellas, and Prepositions" 95
"The Pathfinder's Burden" 108
patron
   point of view 10
Pattee, Fred Lewis 67
"Pattern, Structure, and Conceptualization in Classification" 76
Pease, Theodore Calvin 70
Pennsylvania Magazine of History and Biography 103
"The People, Yes" 95
perforated tapes 14, 25
"On the Permanence of the Invisible" 82
Perry, James W. 18, 20, 26-37, 74, 76, 77
   contribution to librarianship 35
   resignation from Western Reserve University 32
Peterson's Guides 92
Philadelphia Bibliographic Center and Union Library Catalogue 68
Philippine Islands 96
"The Phronemophobic ALA" 94
"The Physician and the Librarian; the Living Body and the Living Word" 103
Physics Today 80, 96
"The Place of Bookbinding in the Library School Curriculum" 78
"The Place of Library Service in Research: a Suggestion" 64

"Playgirl of the Western World" 95
PNLA Quarterly 66
Polushkin, Viktor A. 98
Poole, William Frederick 86
Population Problems 64
population studies *see* Scripps Foundation for Popular Research
Powell, Lawrence C. 79
Predeek, Albert 69
"Preliminary Planning Conference on Information Processing and Correlation" 74
"Present Day Methods for the Storage and Retrieval of Information" 78
"The Present State of Bibliography in the United States; a Condensation of the U.S. Report on National and International Bibliographic Problems" 71
"The Preservation of Local Illinois Newspapers; a Report of the Committee on Local Illinois Newspapers" 72
"President's Message" 99, 100
Press of Case Western Reserve University 72, 75-77, 79, 80-99
Princeton 92
"The Problem of Finance; Working Paper No. 4" 89
Problems of Library School Administration 89
Proceedings of a Conference on Regional Medical Library Service 92
Proceedings of the International Study Conference on Classification in Information Retrieval, Dorking 76
Proceedings of an Invitational Conference 88
Proceedings of the Second International Study Conference held at Hotel Prins Hamlet, Elsinore, Denmark, September 14-18, 1964 91, 92
Proceedings of the Second Library History Seminar, Florida State University Library School, March 4-6, 1965 92

Proceedings of a Work Conference on Bibliographic Control of Newer EducationalMedia 78
Proceedings of the 31st Hearing and Congress of the International Federation for Documentation in Cooperation with the American Documentation Institute, Washington, D.C., October 7-16, 1965 90
"Professional Aspects of Information Science and Technology" 100
"Professionalism and the Socratic Paradox" 42
"Program for Education of Librarians and Documentalists of the Future" 75
"Program for the Stimulation of National Bibliography in the Critical Areas" 72
"Prolegomena to Bibliographic Control" 69
"The Propaedeutic of the New Librarianship" 83
psychometrics 10
Public Librarianship; a Reader 108
punched
 ~ card(s) 15, 25
 ~ sorters 14
  IBM 15
 ~ paper tapes 28
Publications for American Society of Information Sciences 104
pushbutton libraries 25
"Putting Knowledge to Work; the Reaffirmation of a Credo, a Rededication to the Faith" 75

Q

Queens College Press 101
"The Quiet Stir of Thought; or What the Computer Cannot do" 97

R

Rand Development Corporation 29
Rand, Remington 40
Ranganathan, Shivali Ramarita 35, 68, 73, 83, 84
 Ranganathan: a Pattern Maker 104

"Shivali Ramarita Ranganathan" 79
"S. R. Ranganathan; One American View" 83
"S. R. Ranganathan; a Study" 85, 104
Ranz, Joseph 87
rapid selector 16, 17, 18
 see also Shaw, Ralph
Rawski, Conrad H.   93, 95
A Reader in American Library History 99, 103
Reader in the Academic Library 80, 96
"The Readiness is All" 98
"Recent Social Trends and Future Library Policy" 65
"Of Red Carpets and Pruning Shears" 81
Reed, Sarah R.   89
Rees, Alan M.   30, 88, 92
Reference, Research, and Regionalism 90
Reinhold [publisher]   74, 75
"A Renaissance in Library History?" 89
"Report from the ALA Council" 93-95
Report of the United States Delegate to the UNESCO Conference on the Improvement of Bibliographic Services, Paris, France, November 7-10, 1950 71
Report of a Rochester Area Conference on Technology Transfer and Innovation in Business and Industry, 21-24 Rochester, NY 92
"Report of Consultants to the Ad Hoc Committee on the Establishment of a School of Library Studies at the State University of New York at Buffalo" 89
"Report of the Chairman of the Publications Committee of the Rowfant Club, 1977" 105
"Report of the Chairman of the Publications Committee of the Rowfant Club, 1978" 106
Report to the Committee on Guidelines for Medical School Libraries of the Association of American Medical Colleges on *The Future of the Medical School Library* 87
"Report on the Proposed Doctoral Program in the Department of Library Science, School of Graduate Studies, University of Toronto" 98
"The Removal of Shellac and Ink from the Backs of Leather-bound Volumes" 64
"Research and Development in Documentation" 76
"Research and Training in Documentation at Western Reserve University" 75
Research Memorandum on Internal Migration in the Depression 66, 100
Resolution of the Literature Crisis in the Decade 1960-1970 77
"A Review of the Present State of Librarianship and Documentation" 72
Revue de la Documentation 70
Revue Internationale de Documentation 87
Reynolds, Michael M.   80
Rhees, William J.   96
Richardson, John 108
Richmond—and Beyond" 65
Rider, Fremont 82
Robbins-Carter, Jane 108
"Robert S. Taylor"   94
Rogers, Frances   103
"The Role of the College Library: a Reappraisal" 74
The Role of Classification in the Modern American Library   77, 78
Ross, L. A.   2
RQ 87
Rowfant Club Yearbook   105-107
Rub-off 78, 84, 94, 99
Ruderman, Gerald H.
 wife 2
Rufsvold, Margaret I.   78

S

"Salary Survey Endorsed by Tenure Committee"   66
Saturday Review   76

INDEX   123

The Sayers Memorial Volume: Essays in Librarianship in Memory of William CharlesBerwick Sayers 79, 81
Scarecrow Press 72, 82, 83, 99, 102, 103, 106
Schick, Frank L. 94
Schlesinger, Arthur M. 68
"The School of Library Science at Case Western Reserve University" 97
Schrader, Alvin M. 107
Science 93, 94, 104
Scripps Foundation for Popular Research 2, 6, 7, 9, 13, 14, 15
searching selector 28, 32
"Selected Bibliography" 66, 100
"The Self-destructing Diploma" 101
"Second Prize" 65
Sharp, Harold S. 87
Sharp, Henry A. 69
Shaw, Ralph 16, 17, 18, 92
   Director of Libraries at the Department of Agriculture 17
"The Sheepskin Syndrome" 90
Shera, Helen Bickham 7, 13
Sherratt, Andrew 106
Shores, Louis 106
Shoestring Press 81, 102
Siega, Gorgonio D. 96
Silliman University Library 95
Sills, David L. 94
Simonton, Wesley 83
"Sing Me a Song of Social Significance; or, That's Not my Income – That's my Deficit: a Report from ALA Council" 96
SLA *see* Special Libraries Association
Smith, Josephine Metcalf 96
"Social Epistemology, General Semantics, and Libraries" 79, 80
Social Science Research Council 66, 100
The Sociological Foundations of Librarianship 97
"The Sociological Relationships of Information Science" 99
Socratic paradox 42
SOLTAS News 91
"Souse Us in Literature" 101
Spartan Books 90

"Special Librarianship and Documentation" 72
Special Libraries 65, 66, 68, 75, 77, 87, 95
Special Libraries Association – SLA 28, 40, 66, 80, 100
   Bulletin of the Texas Chapter 100
   SLA Newsletter, Cincinnati Chapter 66
"Special Librarianship – How Special?" 100
"Special Libraries; Why 'Special'?" 92
"Special Library Objectives and Their Relation to Administration" 68
"The Spirit Giveth Life; Louis Round Wilson and Chicago's Graduate Library School" 107
The Spirit of Inquiry; the Graduate Library School of Chicago, 1921-1951 108
Sputnik 29, 30
   hysteria 36
Srivastava, Anand P. 104
"S. R. Ranganathan; One American View" 84
"Staffing Library Services to Meet Student Needs – Library Education" 83, 86
"Standard Lists; an Unstandardized View" 93
"Standardizing Language for Machine Searching" 78
State University of New York (SUNY) 98
Stern, Madeline B. 77
Stevens, Norman D. 99, 100, 103
Strategies for Change in Information Programs 100
"The Strength of the Pack" 66
Strout, Donald E. 77, 78
Stoddard, George D. 95, 97
Stravon 95
   ~ Educational Press and Parents' Magazine 97
student
   point of view 10
Student Use of Libraries; an Inquiry into the Needs of Students, Libraries, and the Educational Process 83, 86
Study of Information 109

The Subject Analysis of Library Materials 72
"A Summary of the Historical Background of Classification Theory" 69
"Surplus Books Available from Army and Navy Instructional Programs" 68
Survey of the Saginaw Library System 69
Sutton, Walter 82
"Swan Song of a Junior" 66
Swanson, Rowena W. 94
symbolic interactionism 53-56
Symposium on Post-war Activities 68
Symposium on Special Classification Systems 69
Syracuse University Press 94

T

tabulating machines 13, 14, 15, 17
   see also Hollerith, Herman
   IBM 14, 15
Targets for Research in Library Education 100
Tate, Vernon D. 19
Taube, Mortimer 19, 20
"Taube, Mortimer (1910-1965)" 105
Tauber, Maurice F. 72, 75, 80, 82, 83
Taylor, Margaret S. 69
"On the Teaching of Cataloging" 75
technology
   communication 13, 15, 19
   innovation 25, 39
Texas Library Association 90
"Toward a New Dimension for Library Education" 84
"Toward a Program for Ohio Librarians" 84
Thayer, Lee 50-52, 54
"Theory and Technique in Library Education" 79
"This Could be the Start" 89
Thomas, Dorothy, Dr. 66
Thompson, James 106
Thompson, Kenneth 105
Thompson, Warren S. 6, 7, 8, 9, 64-66, 100, 102
   Director of the Scripps Foundation 2, 6

Thornton, John L. 84, 93
Tomeski, Edward A. 80
"Tomorrow, and Tomorrow, and Tomorrow" 66
"Training for 'Specials': a Prologue to Revision" 66
"Training for 'Specials': the Status of the Library Schools" 66
"The Training of Librarians and Documentalists in the United States" 71
"Training the Chemical Librarian; a Challenge and an Opportunity" 75
"The 'Trickster' in Library Research" 93
"Trusteeship – Trust or Bust?" 85
"Try to Remember" 94
Totten, Herman L. 102
Tully, R. J. 84
"The Turning of the Worm" 88
"Twelve Apostles and a Few Heretics [short version]" 97
"Two Centuries of American Librarianship" 104
"Two Decisive Decades; Documentation into Information Science" 100

U

"The 'Unaffiliated' Member and the SLA" 65
UNESCO 71
   UNESCO Bulletin for Libraries 82, 95
   "The UNESCO Conference on the Improvement of Bibliographic Services" 71
   "The UNESCO Conference on the Improvement of Bibliographic Services; a Preliminary Report" 70
   UNESCO Courier 84, 84
United Educators 86, 98, 99, 102-108
U.S. Department of Health, Education, and Welfare 78, 89
United States Office of Censorship 15
United States Office of Education 28, 78

INDEX

"The United States Report on National and International Bibliographic Problems" 69, 70
United States Research and Development Board 69
Universal Decimal Classification 39
University of Chicago *see* Chicago
University of Illinois 105
University of Karachi 108
University of Minnesota
  Center for Continuation Study 83
"Upon First Looking into John Cook Wyllie's 'The Need'" 96
University of Kansas Press 67
"The Upside-down Library" 106
Urbana, Illinois 105
U.S. Department of State Bulletin 71
user
  ~ orientation 9
  ~ point of view 9, 10
Utah Libraries 106
Utley, George B. 72

V

"On the Value of Library History" 99
"Viewpoint Shift in Reference Work" 65
Vogt, Leona A. 92
Vogt, Melvin J. 99, 101

W

"Walter Brahm Appointed State Librarian of Connecticut" 86
"A Warm Puppy is not Happiness" 86
Warren, G. Garry 108
Washington, D.C. 19, 20, 26, 69, 80, 89, 90, 92, 95, 96, 99, 103
Wedgeworth, Robert 107
Weil, B. H. 74
Wellborn, Fred W. 67
Wells, A.J. 72
Westcott, Richard W. 80
Western Reserve *see* Case Western Reserve
  University
"Western Reserve University Library School"

Western Reserve University, School of Library Science, Academic Year 1661-62 80
"What is a Book that Man May Know It?" 82, 98
"What is Librarianship?" 81, 102
"What Librarianship is of Most Worth?" 95
"What Lies Ahead in Classification" 77, 78
"And What of the Future?" 66
"What the Historian has been Missing" 90
"What's Wrong with Educational Excellence?" 93
Wheels Begin to Turn" 87
"Where is Today's Brother Keppel?" 85
Whirlwind 18
White, Carl M. 104
Whitehill, Walter Muir 75
"For Whom do we Conserve? Or, What can You do With a Gutenberg Bible?" 100
Wiley, Becker & Hayes 97, 100
"William to Tucker to Jess" 87
Williams, Clyde 26
Williams, Martha E. 104
Williamson, William L. 87
Wilson Bulletin 64-67
Wilson Library Bulletin 70, 80-91, 93-96, 99
Wilson Library Journal 92
Wilson, Louis Round 75
Wilson, Pauline 104
"Of Wine, Waiters, and Librarians" 89
Winger, Howard W. 106
Winship, George Parker 68
Winsor, Justin 16
Wisconsin Magazine History 87
"Without Reserve" 99
Woodford, Frank B. 89
Woods, Bill M. 92
Woolf, Edward 103
World Topics Yearbook 86, 98-102, 104, 105, 107, 108
World War II 17, 62
Wright, Curtis H. 42, 104
Wright, Wyllis E. 69
Wroth, Lawrence C. 70

Wyllie, John Cook 70
Wynar, Bohdan S. 105

Y

Yale University 2, 3, 5, 8, 9
"Year for Action" 86
Yearbook of the Institute of General Semantics 79, 80

"Yes, Virginia, There is a Verner Clapp" 83
"You're Going on a Spree in 1973" 93
"Is Youth Rejecting Science?" 89

Z

zatacoding 25